DATE DUE	

A scene from the Playwrights Horizons production of "Fit To Be Tied." Set design by
James Youmans.

Photo by Joan Marcus

FIT TO BE TIED

BY NICKY SILVER

★

★

DRAMATISTS
PLAY SERVICE
INC.

FIT TO BE TIED
is dedicated to T. Scott Cunningham

FIT TO BE TIED was produced by Playwrights Horizons (Tim Sanford, Artistic Director; Leslie Marcus, Managing Director) in New York City, on October 20, 1996. It was directed by David Warren; the set design was by James Youmans; the costume design was by Teresa Snider-Stein; the lighting design was by Donald Holder; the original music and sound design were by John Gromada; the production manager was Chrisopher Boll; and the production stage manager was C.A. Clark. The cast was as follows:

ARLOC .... T. Scott Cunningham
NESSA ....Jean Smart
CARL .... Dick Latessa
BOYD .... Matt Keeslar

ACKNOWLEDGMENT

This Play was written with support from Playwrights Horizons made possible in part by funds granted to the Author through a program sponsored by Amblin Entertainment, Inc.

CHARACTERS

ARLOC — 28. He is attractive, despite his protestations. Arloc is a very troubled person, intelligent, cerebral. He has, at times, the quality of a caged animal.

NESSA — 46. Arloc's mother. A very verbal, flamboyant and self-dramatizing woman. A child herself, she has the sense of being the star in her own comic drama. Dressed in a subdued manner, her clothing is contrary to her true nature. She seems to talk in bursts and sputters. There is a comic edge to her explosive temper.

BOYD — 20s. An overtly sexy young man, cocky in some areas, insecure in others. Uneducated but highly intelligent.

CARL — 50. Nessa's husband. A businessman with an extremely hard shell.

ACT ONE
"Mistakes & Amends"
Thanksgiving week in New York City

ACT TWO
"The New Year"
Three weeks later

FIT TO BE TIED

ACT ONE

"Mistakes & Amends"

Scene 1

The stage is dark. A light comes up on Arloc Simpson. He is in his late twenties and quite attractive, despite his protestations. He addresses the audience, quite agitated.

ARLOC.   DON'T JUDGE ME!! So, I did something terrible?! So what? Everyone's done *something* terrible at some time, haven't they? — and it's not as if I murdered someone or something!!

   (He smiles, tries to compose himself.) I suppose I should introduce myself. I'm Arloc Simpson, but a lot of you probably recognize me from the papers. I was in the papers quite a bit when I was younger. It was terrible. It was after my father died. He was very, very wealthy (his father invented frozen food or something, I don't know. I never knew him and I never paid attention). In any event, my father was rich. And when he died, I was twelve at the time, he left all of his money to me, *not* my mother. He left her nothing, which pissed her off no end. You'll probably recognize her later too. The point is, he left it all to me and she sued me — or the estate actually, but it felt like me — and lost. So our pictures were in the paper and people stared at us wherever we went — OH, JUDGE ME IF YOU WANT! I DON'T CARE — I didn't plan to do it — well, obviously I did plan it — I mean, I bought equipment. I bought supplies — but I didn't plan it for very

long. It's not as if I worked it out over years or anything. The idea just sort of occurred to me one day. It came to me and then before I knew it, it was done. Do you understand?

I'm not arguing insanity. I don't think I was insane. I don't think I am now either — appearances to the contrary. I was perhaps depressed. I'll agree to that: I was depressed. You see, before "this," this incident, I think I only ever knew, I think I only ever *cared for* one other person. And he cared for me. I believe he did. I choose to. Do you understand? And then he died and I will hate him forever. I don't mean that. Yes, I do.

In any event, I think that's when this started. The morning I found out that Anthony died. No one called me. I read it in the paper. And I knew AT ONCE I was in trouble! I knew I'd made a mistake! But before Anthony, I had waited forever. I had waited MY WHOLE LIFE to be with someone, to let someone look at me! And I did NOT care what was dangerous! I DIDN'T CARE about myself! About me! I ONLY CARED THAT I HAD WAITED FOREVER!... It started that night, when I read he was gone. I couldn't sleep. My muscles hurt. I read Anthony's obituary over and over again in my head — PNEUMONIA is a code word when you read it in the paper! I'M NOT STUPID!... I offered up my blood at noon and met my mother for lunch at twelve thirty.

(*Light comes up revealing a restaurant, actually a single table in front of an act curtain. Nessa is seated and applying lipstick, using her knife as a mirror. She is quite attractive and dressed elegantly. Her only jewelry is a wedding ring and a strand of pearls. There is a basket of bread and a bottle of wine. Nessa drinks throughout the scene.*)

NESSA. You're late.

ARLOC. (*Joining her.*) I'm not.

NESSA. I've been here forever. This was a Laundromat when I arrived. Now it's a bistro. I know you enjoy torturing me, Arloc, but I was hoping we could keep it behind closed doors.

ARLOC. How are you mother?

NESSA. I'm fine. I'm very well.

ARLOC. I barely recognize you.

NESSA.   Don't make fun of me. I've lightened my hair a shade. That's all.

ARLOC.   Oh?

NESSA.   And I've lost a little weight.

ARLOC.   I see.

NESSA.   And fine! Fine! I had my eyes done!

ARLOC.   I thought so.

NESSA.   And I had some fat sucked out from under my chin — strictly in-patient. Dr. Halpern says it's entirely too soon for a complete lift, but bits of maintenance postpone the inevitable.

ARLOC.   You're tan.

NESSA.   Carl and I were on St. Bart's last week! I did some water skiing — I did some *scuba diving!* Can you believe it? Me? At my age? With one of those oxygen tank-things strapped on my back. Keep going, keep going: that's the secret. It was stunning! The vistas!

ARLOC.   Well, I'm glad you enjoyed —

NESSA.   Of course I broke all of my nails. These are acrylic.

ARLOC.   You look ... well —

NESSA.   Thank you —

ARLOC.   Artificial.

NESSA.   I detest you.

ARLOC.   I know.

NESSA.   Do you want some wine?

ARLOC.   No.

NESSA.   It's very good. Why were you late?

ARLOC.   I was shopping.

NESSA.   Christmas?

ARLOC.   The crowds.

NESSA.   Did you buy me a present?

ARLOC.   Of course not.

NESSA.   What could I be thinking? When did you *ever* buy me a present?

ARLOC.   As I recall, when I was nineteen, I bought you a car.

NESSA.   But it was a *bad* car, Arloc! It was very small and the tape thing kept eating all the.... things — tapes. I hated that car. And that was years ago. You have a list of my sizes, don't you?

ARLOC. *(Irritated.)* Yes.

NESSA. What's wrong? What's wrong with you? What is it? Are you in a mood?

ARLOC. I'm not. I'm moodless. I'm blank.

NESSA. *(Lighting a cigarette.)* God!!! How do you do it!? You leave me stranded here for hours, for years — I was fifteen when I got here — and you put me on the defensive! I don't understand it!

ARLOC. Did you order?

NESSA. Just the wine. He said he'll be back —

ARLOC. Do you have to smoke?

NESSA. No. No. Obviously, I don't HAVE to. I don't have to smoke — I can chew gum like some kind of third rate *chorine* if you'd prefer! I could chew tobacco!

ARLOC. I don't think you're even allowed to smoke —

NESSA. I don't HAVE to have a cigarette, but my lungs are used to it! Do you understand? My system *expects* a certain amount of tar and nicotine shoveled into it every day. But why concern yourself with my needs? When did you ever? I won't smoke. Alright! Happy? I'll put it out. But don't be embarrassed if I should start gagging, writhing in nicotine withdrawal, on the floor, like a rabid dog thrashing about in the middle of lunch and you have to pay for the crystal and the flatware and the broken dishes —

ARLOC. FINE! Smoke! I don't need to taste anything. Smoke all you want and shorten your life! See if I care!!

NESSA. *(After a moment.)* Do you want one?

ARLOC. No!

NESSA. Suit yourself.

ARLOC. What do you want? Why have I been "summoned?"

NESSA. Are you coming to dinner next week?

ARLOC. Will Carl be there?

NESSA. He's my husband.

ARLOC. I have plans.

NESSA. It's Thanksgiving.

ARLOC. I'm aware.

NESSA. I can't imagine why you hate Carl.

ARLOC. I can't imagine that you don't.

NESSA. He's a wonderful man.

ARLOC. He has asked me to call him "Daddy."

NESSA. He likes you.

ARLOC. I didn't call my father Daddy.

NESSA. He makes me very happy.

ARLOC. You are the Picasso of self-delusion.

NESSA. Carl and I are perfect together. We laugh constantly! We can't have a conversation without dissolving into fits of laughter like imbeciles.

ARLOC. I'm glad you're happy.

NESSA. *(Hostile.)* Happy!? At night I hold a pillow over his face! His moist, squishy, horrible face! He's off red meat. He *exercises*. Rides a thing. A bicycle thing — He's in very good shape for a hundred and ten — His breathing gives me headaches! His even, measured, rhythmic breath: in/out, in/out till I could scream!

ARLOC. I do not understand why you don't just —

NESSA. You think you're so superior! You think it's so much better being alone? It's not easy for me.

ARLOC. Don't! Start!

NESSA. I'm sorry. We'll talk about something else — I HAVE NO SKILLS! I'm ornamental! I'm like one of those Stuben animals. Nice to look at but without function. I could be a paperweight!

ARLOC. Please.

NESSA. Hang me from a tree at Christmas.

ARLOC. You have hidden skills. You must.

NESSA. I can't do a thing. And it *is* a grind. The days are so long. The days are centuries. How do you fill your days, Arloc? People ask me about you.

ARLOC. Who?

NESSA. People. People. People ask me, "How's Arloc?"

ARLOC. People? Who are these people.

NESSA. People. Friends. You know. Carl's friends. They say, "What's Arloc up to?" I don't know what to tell them. I lie. I used to say you were in the army, but no one believed that.

No one who's met you, because — well, because, you know. It's obvious.

ARLOC.   I do hate you.

NESSA.   Now I say you're doing charity work. I say you sit on committees. What committees, I've no idea. I tell them you read pornographic novels to the blind.

ARLOC.   Tell them it's none of their business.

NESSA.   What do you *do?*

ARLOC.   I read. I write. I go for walks. I think.

NESSA.   About what?

ARLOC.   Reading, writing and going for walks.

NESSA.   Your lethargy is pathological, Arloc. You need an interest. The mind is a muscle, and yours is going to atrophy. I know because mine is mashed potatoes. You're going to end up selling imitation Rolex watches from a card table outside of Sak's.

ARLOC.   Can we *please* talk about something else?

NESSA.   The Jennings, whom we saw in St. Bart's, have a son.

ARLOC.   Please don't. I still get letters from the last one.

NESSA.   He was very nice.

ARLOC.   Letters from prison!

NESSA.   The Jennings boy is perfect for you!

ARLOC.   *(Shouting.)* I'm not interested!!

NESSA.   His name is Brandon. Here's his number. *(She hands him a business card.)*

ARLOC.   *(Quite upset.)* Was this the reason for our lunch? Please tell me. Your chatter is giving me a headache.

NESSA.   *(After a moment.)* I need some money.

ARLOC.   I sent you your check.

NESSA.   I know, thank you. I need some extra.

ARLOC.   What for?

NESSA.   *(Composure cracking.)* Why do you have to embarrass me like this? Do you have any idea how degrading this is? How humiliating?

ARLOC.   You're a grown-up.

NESSA.   *(Falling apart.)* That's right, I am. I'm a grown-up and I have to grovel like a thing, a child or a dottering old person *incapable* of anything. It's a terrible, terrible — I HAVE

A KNOT IN MY STOMACH THE SIZE OF A MELON. God! I dread these conversations. It's Christmas and I need a little help and WHY IS THERE NO MORE WINE?! Tell me that, would you?

ARLOC. (*Contrite.*) You asked me. You're not groveling. I'm sorry. Really.

NESSA. I wish I were dead!! I do. Just humiliation after humiliation. It's more than I can take! I should throw myself into traffic! I leave everything to you. I DON'T HAVE A GODDAMN THING, nothing in the world to call my own, but it's yours. All of it. All my dresses! Let them out, take them up. Do what you want. They're yours.

ARLOC. Can't you ask Carl?

NESSA. We've been through this. And through this and through this.

ARLOC. He's your husband.

NESSA. (*Bursting.*) You know how he is. He's bitter and mercenary. And distrustful — GOD, HE'S MADE OF MARBLE! Terrified of feelings — I mean Adelle died *twenty* years ago and he's still angry! He calls out at night in his sleep, and it's not *my* name he calls! He has issues. Issues! Issues! Everywhere you look! Issues! You can't get in the house for them!

ARLOC. You know what I think —

NESSA. I apologize. I'm sorry. I'm sorry. This is so perverse! I'm your mother. I shouldn't unburden myself on you. I want to help you. Will you call whatever-his-name-is, that boy? You know. Whomever. Whatever.

ARLOC. No.

NESSA. I am sorry I exploded. I am. Lately things have been — you look very well, really — NOT GOOD! Things have been NOT GOOD. But you know: rough smooth, rough smooth.

ARLOC. You should just leave Carl and stop complaining.

NESSA. It's very hard —

ARLOC. Do you think it's pleasant, do you think I enjoy seeing you this miserable!?

NESSA. Frankly?

ARLOC. Don't be ridiculous! You should just leave him and

if you won't do that, if you won't help yourself —

NESSA.   I HATE YOUR FATHER! HE DID THIS TO ME! HE CONDEMNED US TO THIS MOCKERY —

ARLOC.   It's not his fault.

NESSA.   HE REDUCED ME TO THIS!

ARLOC.   If you hadn't been so completely promiscuous —

NESSA.   I cannot imagine it is even *remotely* appropriate for you say such things to me! I am, after all, your mother! You came out of my womb! And if, at the moment, or even in the long run, I seem to be somewhat less than functional, you have no business taking advantage of that!! I have made sacrifices and lived a less than charmed life in order to merely survive! WHERE IS THE FUCKING WAITER!

ARLOC.   LISTEN! LISTEN TO ME! IF YOU LEAVE HIM, I WILL HELP YOU! I WILL TAKE CARE OF YOU! JUST DO IT AND FOR GOD'S SAKE STOP TALKING ABOUT IT! ALRIGHT!

NESSA.   *(After a long pause.)* Well ... Arloc ... there's no need to shout. Point taken.... Let's order. Shall we? *(Blackout.)*

Scene 2

A pool of light comes up on Arloc. As he speaks the general lighting comes up very slowly, never reaching full. We see, dimly, his apartment, which is vast and furnished in a manner suggesting an older inhabitant: Chippendale chairs, Oriental rugs. There is a Matisse cut-out on one wall, and a window, beyond which we can see New York City.

ARLOC.   Several days later the phone rings and a doctor on the other end asks for Arloc Simpson. I tell him not to speak. I DON'T WANT TO KNOW! The words will float in space like tangible things, pieces of dirt in the air —   DON'T SPEAK THEM! PLEASE DON'T SAY THEM! I am mailed a letter that I can *not* open. *(He produces a sealed letter from his jacket pocket.)* It's my enemy. I put it here, on this table, on a magazine, beneath a paperweight. And my apartment is too small for both of us. So I leave — I PLANNED NOTHING! Do you understand? I leave. I walk. I walk and walk, sweating in the cold November air. I go into churches. I go into stores and theaters.... And then I see ... *him. (Abruptly, the general light and Arloc's go out, as a light comes up on Nessa, who addresses the audience.)*

NESSA.   I met Arloc's father when I was seventeen years old. Bennett was fifty, rich as Midas. And I got pregnant. Oh, glass houses, glass houses. I met Carl at Bennett's funeral. Carl's first wife, Adelle — a wealthy British import he met at "the club" — was killed quite randomly, twenty years ago in a traffic accident, the details of which escape me. But there rests on a table in our foyer, a shrine: her ashes in an urn. Which I use to extinguish cigarettes. I'm afraid I smoke to excess and have had to empty the urn from time to time, so I cannot imagine there is much of her left. I smoke in bed and dream, all the time, of telling Carl it's over, that I am leaving him. In my dream he's on one of his "machines." *(Light comes up on Carl walking on a machine.)* And we say wonderfully nasty, terrible things to each other. *(She joins Carl.)* We have to talk.

CARL.   Philip Cunningham died today.

NESSA.   You're obsessed with dying, Carl.

CARL.   Six months younger than me and, just like that, the man goes down.

NESSA.   You're going to die one of these days.

CARL.   No, I'm not. Not me.

NESSA.   Of course you are.

CARL.   Not as long a I keep walking.

NESSA.   I would appreciate it Carl, if you would just *stop* walking and die!

CARL.   I'm not going to die to suit you.

NESSA.   I was afraid of that. You know I hate you.

CARL.   I do.

NESSA.   The day I married you was my funeral! My bridesmaids were pallbearers!

CARL.   You're drunk!

NESSA.   I screwed Peter Cunningham!

15

CARL. His name was Philip —

NESSA. We didn't need names!

CARL. You're an alcoholic, Nessa!

NESSA. We clawed at each other and fucked like wild dogs!

CARL. You should be in a clinic!

NESSA. We laughed at you behind your back!

CARL. You should be in a home!

NESSA. It's over you bastard!

CARL. You should be in a hospital!

NESSA. I'm leaving you!

CARL. I'm thrilled!

NESSA. I'm going to sue your ass into oblivion!

CARL. Money well spent to be free!

NESSA. Good bye!

CARL. Get out!

NESSA. *(Out.)* That is how I dream it. *(Their light goes out. Arloc's returns.)*

ARLOC. He was beautiful! He was to me! To me, he was! I had to see him. I had to tell him. I wanted to look at him all the time! I had to touch him! I had to smell him! I had to hear him say my name! BUT I DIDN'T MEAN TO DO ANYTHING WRONG! I walked every day! Every night! Surrounded by families, not speaking English, squalling children, smelling sticky, not understanding, never noticing what was in front of them! I understood — I watched the way he moved! I watched his hands in the air, floating, flying, swooping in the sky made of blue construction paper. And every time I left my home I passed IT — that envelope that held my fate — I saw him everywhere! He was everywhere I looked! Him, with no name! Him with soft hair! Him with his lips and his voice! Him loving me! And every night, alone in my bed, WE made love! And I whispered his name into my pillow — Sean, Philip, Daniel, Danny, Dan — I started to prepare! *(Arloc's light goes out, Nessa's comes up, she is standing at a chart which indicates the following.)*

NESSA. *(Instructional.)* We have breakfast every morning at seven, after Carl runs. We see one of his children, alternately, on the first Sunday of each month. Carl wears a blue suit on

Monday, a gray one on Tuesday, a striped one on Wednesday, another gray one on Thursday and another blue one on Friday, but they all look the same to me. He swims on Tuesdays. Tennis on Thursdays. Golf on Sundays, unless we're seeing his children, Scott and Audrey. We have dinner every night at seven-thirty, no red meat, no white flour, no white sugar, not much flavor, and have perfunctory sex every Saturday. Until recently. The last year or so. *(A light comes up on Carl.)*

CARL.   Are you coming? The reservation is for seven-thirty.

NESSA.   I'm coming. I just have to finish my —

CARL.   You know I hate being late. There's *nothing* more important in life, than a schedule.

NESSA.   Yes, I know. *(Carl's light goes out.)* There's not enough liquor in the world. *(Nessa's light goes out. Arloc's returns.)*

ARLOC.   I DIDN'T THINK ABOUT IT! I JUST DID IT! Then one day, one night days later, I waited on the street. I waited where they come out into the world — HE SAW ME! I KNOW HE DID! And I heard something, I heard someone call his name. His name was Boyd. He had a name! And I whispered it into my pillow, damp with my sweat, and my saliva! I imagined him, holding him, tasting him, running my tongue over his skin, his jaw, his lips, his nipples — BUT BELIEVE ME! I DIDN'T KNOW HOW THINGS WOULD HAPPEN! — Anyway, in any event, the point is, finally, I asked him, not breathing, after weeks and decades, shaking with nerves, drenched in sweat, if he was free ... after "work." And he said, and I couldn't believe it.... "Yes."

Scene 3

The general lighting comes up abruptly, revealing Boyd seated on the sofa. He is dressed, from head to toe as an angel, white tights, white draped tunic, beautiful wings. His coat is thrown over an arm of the sofa.

ARLOC.   So. Tell me. Boyd. Do you "enjoy" being an angel?

BOYD.   It's a horrible, unending nightmare.

ARLOC.   Really? — I'm sorry, would you like some wine?

BOYD.   No thank you.

ARLOC.   You're sure?

BOYD.   Yes.

ARLOC.   I hate to drink alone.

BOYD.   I don't really —

ARLOC.   Just one?

BOYD.   Alright, fine.

ARLOC.   I have some chilled. *(Arloc exits. Boyd rushes to his coat and gets some pills from his pocket. He gulps two, then quickly looks around. Arloc re-enters, with two glasses of wine and Boyd lurches to a "casual" stance. Handing Boyd a glass.)* Here you go.

BOYD.   Thank you.

ARLOC.   I'm surprised.

BOYD.   By what?

ARLOC.   I would think it'd be fun — flying. I'd think it'd be nice, a pleasant job to have.

BOYD.   The harness leaves red welts on my groin.

ARLOC.   Oh.... It's very beautiful though, Radio City. I'd never been there before. It's very festive. And your costume is … "angelic."

BOYD.   Sorry I couldn't change, but I had to get outa there. I owe The Nutcracker twenty bucks and he's a viscous queen who'd just as soon cut off my balls as look at me.

ARLOC.   Don't apologize. You look very nice. Dignified and seraphic.

BOYD.   Please. I'm in the Christmas Spectacular, not *Perestrioka.*

ARLOC.   Well, it's very becoming.

BOYD.   They spray glitter on these wings, which I believe is completely toxic. Half the angels have emphysema.

ARLOC.   Oh?

BOYD.   You can't hear them hacking in the house?

ARLOC.   No.

BOYD.   It's loud as hell on stage. I bet all the angels die by thirty.

ARLOC.   That's disturbing. You do your line very well —

BOYD.   What line?

18

ARLOC.   You know, when you say, *(Simply.)* "Fear not. For behold I bring you tidings of great joy, which shall be to all people. For unto you is born this day in the city of David, a savior, which is Christ the Lord. And this shall be a sign to you. You shall find the babe wrapped in swaddling clothes ... lying in a manger."

BOYD.   That's not me.

ARLOC.   What?

BOYD.   That's on tape. None of us speak. I just flap my wings so you look my direction.

ARLOC.   Well, I think you're very good.

BOYD.   Are you an agent or something?

ARLOC.   No, but I know. I can tell. I was in plays in school. I was in *The Cherry Orchard*. And I was in *Long Day's Journey Into Night*. I played Mary Tyrone — It was a boys' school.

BOYD.   Oh.

ARLOC.   And you have real talent.

BOYD.   Thanks. Do you live here all alone?

ARLOC.   Yes.

BOYD.   Everything looks so expensive, I'm afraid to touch it.

ARLOC.   Touch anything.

BOYD.   *(He picks up the paperweight.)* What's this?

ARLOC.   Just a paperweight.

BOYD.   Crystal?

ARLOC.   Yes.

BOYD.   I'll put it down.

ARLOC.   Thank you. *(Pause.)* So tell me, Boyd, would I have seen you in anything else — aside from the Christmas Spectacular. Which does seem to be, well, seasonal.

BOYD.   No. I'm not an actor. I just answered an ad.

ARLOC.   What do you do?

BOYD.   I want to make films. I want to be a filmmaker.

ARLOC.   Really? What kind of films?

BOYD.   Documentaries or small, independent films maybe. I figure a couple of seasons at Radio City'll pay for a couple of days at NYU film school.

ARLOC.   Can't your parents help you?

BOYD.   They're dead.

ARLOC. I'm sorry.

BOYD. I think.

ARLOC. Pardon?

BOYD. I think they're dead.

ARLOC. You're not sure?

BOYD. Not really.

ARLOC. Are they very dull?

BOYD. What?

ARLOC. Forget it.

BOYD. I never knew my father.

ARLOC. That could be lucky.

BOYD. My mother left when I was six. I was raised by foster parents, in Asbury Park.

ARLOC. That's terrible.

BOYD. You've been to Asbury Park?

ARLOC. I have.

BOYD. Then you know — *(He falls abruptly into a deep sleep. Arloc is confused at first. He thinks this is perhaps a joke. Then he's shocked. He looks about nervously.)*

ARLOC. Boyd?... Boyd. Oh my God. BOYD!! *(Boyd wakes up.)*

BOYD. What?

ARLOC. Are you alright?

BOYD. Shit.

ARLOC. Do you feel alright?

BOYD. It happened. Didn't it? Shit. Shit! Shit!!

ARLOC. You passed out!

BOYD. I'm fine. I am.

ARLOC. You're sure?

BOYD. I just fell asleep.

ARLOC. Like that?

BOYD. I fall asleep.

ARLOC. I see.

BOYD. I'm sorry.

ARLOC. It's OK.

BOYD. I'm so embarrassed.

ARLOC. Are you sick?

BOYD. I have narcolepsy.

ARLOC. Do you have seizures?

20

BOYD. That's epilepsy. I just fall asleep all of a sudden.

ARLOC. It was very abrupt, you were in the middle —

BOYD. There's scar tissue on my brain which causes pressure. I was a forceps baby.

ARLOC. So was I.

BOYD. It showed up when I was twelve.

ARLOC. I had no adverse reaction.

BOYD. I take pills.

ARLOC. Not often enough.

BOYD. They don't always work. They work perfectly well for a while and then I develop a tolerance for them or something. And it's the wine. I don't usually drink because it effects the medicine. — You won't tell anyone will you?

ARLOC. Who would I tell?

BOYD. Radio City. You won't tell them, will you?

ARLOC. Why would I?

BOYD. I got fired from my last job when they found out.

ARLOC. Where was that?

BOYD. At a day care center.

ARLOC. *(Disturbed by this.)* Oh.

BOYD. See, I never finished school — My foster parents were complete idiots and they pulled me out when I was nine. To work — They had this act in a club on the Boardwalk. The Salt and Pepper Review — (From the name you'd assume one of them was black. They weren't. They were white. Both of them — total morons.) They sang standards in wrong tempos: I hated the show, so I refused to learn "Glad to Be Unhappy" as a syncopated cha-cha and ran away when I was twelve. I ended up at Grand Central.

ARLOC. At twelve?

BOYD. I wandered around the station wishing on the stars painted on the ceiling. That was the first time I fell asleep — I mean abruptly, because of my condition. I woke up in the men's room, half naked and relieved of what little money I'd had. I opened my eyes to a very old man with long white hair. I thought I'd died and he was God. I told him I had run away and I was moving into the third stall. So he took me home and fed me and I stayed there for six years. He took care of me and took me to doctors. He taught me at home and bought me presents. Then a social worker came, and finding us in bed she threatened to remove me. So my third father climbed to the roof and let himself fall. *(He falls asleep again, abruptly. Arloc moves quietly next to him. He kneels next to Boyd and speaks softly.)*

ARLOC. You're so beautiful. Boyd ... I love you. Don't be angry. I don't even know you and I don't know why and I don't care what pathology there is in me that makes it so ... *(He touches Boyd's face very lightly. Boyd does not stir.)* I love you.... Do you love me?... You'll stay here. You can stay here. Forever. You'll be with me.... And afterwards. I'll take care of you. Make your movies.... Do you love me?... Do you?... Boyd!! *(Boyd wakes up. Arloc sits back.)*

BOYD. Shit. Shit. Shit. It happened again, didn't it?

ARLOC. Yes.

BOYD. It's the wine. You must think I'm pathetic.

ARLOC. Not at all —

BOYD. I think I should be going. When it gets like this. I have to sleep for an hour.

ARLOC. Please don't —

BOYD. Then I'm fine.

ARLOC. Can I kiss you?

BOYD. What?

ARLOC. *(Standing.)* You're very beautiful.

BOYD. Thank you.

ARLOC. *(After a moment.)* You're supposed to say I'm nice looking.

BOYD. Oh.

ARLOC. Or words to that effect.

BOYD. You're nice looking.

ARLOC. Thank you ... I know I'm not, by the way. But I have other fine qualities, which may not be apparent at the moment. Can I kiss you? Just once.

BOYD. Yes. *(Arloc kisses him. It is gentle, not sexual.)*

ARLOC. Thank you.

BOYD. Well, it was nice meeting you.

ARLOC. Stay.

BOYD. I can't.

ARLOC. Why not?

BOYD. I should go.

ARLOC. Why?

BOYD. I ought to.

ARLOC. Can I see you again?

BOYD. Sure.

ARLOC. Tomorrow?

BOYD. I can't.

ARLOC. Please?

BOYD. I'm sorry.

ARLOC. Don't go.

BOYD. I have to.

ARLOC. Please.

BOYD. I'm sorry.

ARLOC. Ten minutes.

BOYD. I can't.

ARLOC. Ten minutes! Just stay ten more minutes! OK? Just
— we'll chat for ten more minutes. Let me finish my wine.
Please? OK? Please? *(Boyd acquiesces and sits down.)* Thank you.
(Arloc sits.) So. Boyd. Can I tie you up?

BOYD. What!?

ARLOC. Can I tie you up?

BOYD. Are you insane?

ARLOC. I'd like to tie you up.

BOYD. I really have to go.

ARLOC. I don't want to hurt you.

BOYD. It was very nice meeting you.

ARLOC. I'll pay you.

BOYD. I don't do that! I'm not a whore!

ARLOC. I didn't mean to offend you.

BOYD. I have to go —

ARLOC. Five hundred dollars?

BOYD. You're sick.

ARLOC. Don't be such a coward.

BOYD. I'm not a coward! I'm just not insane!

ARLOC. It'll be fun.

BOYD. For you!

ARLOC.   It's thrilling. You give yourself up. You're not a person. You're an object, a sex toy! Haven't you wanted, at some point in your life, to be something else? To be anything else, other than you? Try it. I can do what I want and you'll see, you'll want me to. It's beautiful: the absence of will, the lack of control. Try it. Five minutes. That's all. Here — *(He holds out five hundred dollar bills.)* A hundred dollars a minute.... That's all I'm asking. Five minutes. You'll beg for ten. Trust me, Boyd. I wouldn't hurt you. Ever.

BOYD.   What if I don't like it?

ARLOC.   You say so. I let you go.

BOYD.   I don't know. *(Arloc puts the money into Boyd's pocket.)*

ARLOC.   Try it.

BOYD.   *(After a moment.)* Five minutes.

ARLOC.   Thank you! *(Arloc rushes out of the room.)*

BOYD.   What are you —

ARLOC.   *(Offstage.)* Getting the stuff! *(Boyd rushes to the bar and holds the paperweight. After a moment of internal debate, He stuffs it into the pocket of his coat. Arloc re-enters carrying several pieces of heavy rope and a "bondage chair.")* What are you doing?

BOYD.   Nothing.

ARLOC.   You're not leaving —

BOYD.   I was just getting something —

ARLOC.   You're going to love this! *(He wheels the chair into the center of the room.)* Sit here.

BOYD.   That looks ... severe.

ARLOC.   I got it from a catalogue.

BOYD.   Oh.

ARLOC.   Hands please. *(Boyd sits. Arloc starts to tie him to the chair. It is important that Arloc tie him around the chest and waist, leaving his lower legs free, allowing Boyd to travel but not free himself.)* Now, we'll need a control word.

BOYD.   A what?

ARLOC.   A control word: a word to say if you want me to stop, if I'm really hurting you.

BOYD.   I assume "Stop," would lack the theatrical subterfuge.

ARLOC.   You'll want to say stop anyway. It's part of the experience. *(He looks around.)* How about "Matisse?"

BOYD.   Do you do this often?

ARLOC.   Frankly, I've never done it before.

BOYD.   What?

ARLOC.   This is my first foray into the world of sado-masochism. But how hard could it be?

BOYD.   You led me to believe —

ARLOC.   I never actually said I'd done it.

BOYD.   You implied it!

ARLOC.   You inferred it.

BOYD.   I didn't.

ARLOC.   You did.

BOYD.   Arloc, it's too tight.

ARLOC.   How tight is too tight?

BOYD.   Loosen it.

ARLOC.   Stop whining.

BOYD.   It's too tight.

ARLOC.   It has to be.

BOYD.   This tight?

ARLOC.   Yes, yes, yes.

BOYD.   It hurts.

ARLOC.   Stop fidgeting.

BOYD.   I don't want to do this.

ARLOC.   Don't worry. I don't have any whips or anything.

BOYD.   I don't want to do this!!

ARLOC.   You took my money!

BOYD.   I'll give it back!!

ARLOC.   No thank you.

BOYD.   Arloc, come on. *(Arloc is finished tying him to the chair.)*

ARLOC.   Finished! Try and get away.

BOYD.   Untie me! Untie me this minute!

ARLOC.   Be quiet.

BOYD.   The rope is too tight! It's cutting into me! Into my skin!

ARLOC.   Because you're squirming.

BOYD.   Let me out, I won't squirm!

ARLOC.   No.

BOYD.   Arloc! Stop this! I WANT TO LEAVE! UNTIE ME!

ARLOC.   What's the control word?

BOYD. I don't know!

ARLOC. Of course you do —

BOYD. MATISSE! IT'S MATISSE! NOW UNTIE ME!

ARLOC. ... No.

BOYD. YOU'RE CRAZY!

ARLOC. Don't say that!

BOYD. YOU'RE FUCKING INSANE! THIS HURTS! YOU'RE OUT OF YOUR FUCKING MIND! I DON'T KNOW WHAT YOU WANT, BUT I AM TELLING YOU TO LET ME GO!

ARLOC. I HAVEN'T DONE ANYTHING —

BOYD. SICK FUCKING BASTARD —

ARLOC. STOP IT!

BOYD. YOU'RE SICK! YOU'RE A SICK MOTHERFUCKING —

ARLOC. STOP IT!!!!! *(He grabs a hunk of feathers from Boyd's wings and stuffs it in Boyd's mouth, as a gag. He ties rope around Boyd's head to secure it. Boyd squirms, pointlessly.)* STOP IT! STOP IT! Please! Please ... please. *(There is a long pause while they look at each other. Boyd realizes he is in real trouble. Arloc kneels at Boyd's feet.)* Boyd. Don't say that. Please. Listen to me. Don't struggle, please. Just listen. I won't hurt you. I wouldn't. Do you understand? I will never hurt you ... I love you. I won't touch you, I won't ever touch you. And I will never ... make you touch me. Ever. Just listen. Please. I want someone here. That's all. I want *you* here. You can't leave me, please. It won't be forever. Maybe years — I don't know. But you'll like me. You'll see. I'll help you. I'll give you anything you want. Trust me, Boyd, you never have to go back. You can be anything, anything you want. Just stay here, please, with me. You might someday understand and not hate me, or love me too. Give me a chance. *(There is a knock at the door. Boyd squirms and makes small noises. Arloc goes to the door and looks through the peephole.)* Oh my God! Shit. Shit. Fuck. Damn. Damn. *(Arloc looks about in a frenzy. He has an idea. He drags Boyd, on the chair into his bedroom. He speaks to Boyd in hushed, but wild tones.)* Don't make any noise. Trust me. Don't. Do you understand? *(Having deposited Boyd in the other room, Arloc goes to the bar and searches wildly for something. He finds a set of keys. He runs to the bedroom door and has to try several before he finds the one that locks the door. All the while there is more knocking at the front door.)* Coming! *(Having locked the bedroom shut, he pulls himself together for a beat. Then he opens the door to reveal Nessa, somewhat drunk, dressed tastefully, wearing her pearls.)*

NESSA. I'VE DONE IT!

ARLOC. Mother!!?

NESSA. I've left Carl!!

ARLOC. What?! *(Nessa enters.)*

NESSA. I did. I did it. I've done it — What took you so long to answer the door?

ARLOC. I wasn't dressed — What are you doing here?

NESSA. I've left him. Do you hear me? I feel a huge weight, I feel a mountain, Vesuvius has been lifted from my shoulders. I feel younger! Do I look younger? I feel lighter. Fix me a drink, would you? Vodka please. I'm ready to start over, to be a girl again. Pigtails and freckles. Everything!

ARLOC. This isn't a good time —

NESSA. I can do it too, Arloc! I can be eighteen years old and fresh out of high school.

ARLOC. Maybe you could come back —

NESSA. *(Shedding her coat.)* I am ready to begin my life! I am naked as a newborn, having shed the ill-fitting dress of my marriage!

ARLOC. *(Handing Nessa a drink.)* Here.

NESSA. Thank you — I am standing at an intersection! It's true, a great intersection with ten thousand highways!

ARLOC. Stop talking in metaphors! *(As Nessa downs her drink, he checks the bedroom door and is satisfied that it's secure.)*

NESSA. *(Bitter.)* I wish I were dead. My life is over. I should just smash this glass and open a vein.

ARLOC. You're drunk.

NESSA. I'M NOT DRUNK!! I wish I were. I must've been when I signed my death warrant. I'm going to be alone forever! Look at me! I'm a wizened, withered relic. I belong in the Museum of Natural History. Look at my hands! Are these the hands of a young person? — My God! I'm wearing gloves — it looks like I'm wearing gloves, tweed gloves a size too big. Why can't they tighten the skin on your hands? Tell me that.

27

ARLOC. I don't know.

NESSA. They tighten everything else — Did you know Miriam Taylor had her armpits tightened? It's true! She was unhappy with her look in a sleeveless so she had her armpits tightened! HER ARMPITS! Tight as drums — now she can't lower her arms. People think she's signaling ships — I HATE MY HANDS! Let's cut them off. Do you have a knife? We'll sever the talons and send them to Carl in a gift wrapped box from Bergdorf Goodman's! — No, no, no. No, no. I have got to be positive. I will be. I am a valuable person. I have intrinsic value — Refill — "I have intrinsic value." That's my mantra.

ARLOC. Why are you here?

NESSA. I didn't know where else to go. I took a taxi. The driver thought I was mad. I couldn't catch my breath. I couldn't stop laughing — except when I was crying. You said you'd help me! *(Arloc refills her glass.)*

ARLOC. This isn't really an appropriate time. *(Nessa downs her drink.)*

NESSA. YOU PROMISED ME! YOU MADE ME A PROMISE! You cannot renege now. I should think you'd be sending off Roman candles, doing cartwheels or something. You're the one, Arloc. You are the one.

ARLOC. I'm the one what?

NESSA. You've been pushing and nagging and begging me for years to leave him. You're the one who's framed my marriage in the language of Greek Tragedy. You ought to be thrilled. I am taking control of my life. At last!

ARLOC. I am happy. It's just —

NESSA. Making changes. I'm taking a huge step, a leap really. And I'm counting on you to catch me. — What kind of vodka is this? It's very good.

ARLOC. It's Scotch. I don't have any vodka.

NESSA. It's very good. I like it.

ARLOC. Why are you *here*? What, exactly, do you want?

NESSA. I've done it! Are you there?!! Are you listening?!! I've left Carl. You were right about him. All along. He's really not a very warm person, you know. Last night, last night EVERYTHING became perfectly clear! We were at a Christmas party, something for the bank. I don't know. There was a psychic there, for entertainment. A young girl named Magnolia or Blossom or Tulip or something. And do you know what she said? Of course you don't. I'll tell you. She looked at Carl and she said, "You have no aura." That's it! That's what she said. She told my husband he was *without aura! SANS* aura!! — Refill please.

ARLOC. I think you've had enough.

NESSA. Carl and I used to have sex at the same hour, in the same position (me on top, doing all the work), on the same day for fourteen years! Now NOTHING! A YEAR OF NOTHING! No interest! All he's interested in is his DIET! He's off salt! He's off white flour! He sprinkles brewers yeast on everything! — just a little one?

ARLOC. No!

NESSA. You're too strict. You're mean! — I refuse, absolutely, to end up with nothing again! I thought, if I could catch him with someone — I introduced him to Cynthia Sayer, you know she'd sleep with a Coke bottle if it had a dollar. SHE GOT NOWHERE!

ARLOC. I hate to say it, but I think that's admirable.

NESSA. THAT IS NOT THE POINT! YOU HAVE MISSED THE POINT ENTIRELY!!

ARLOC. You can't assume that because you have affairs, *everyone* is amoral.

NESSA. You never said one nice thing about him in fifteen years and tonight you decide you're allies! I think that's very bad timing, Arloc. Do you think I can start over? Do you? Or do you think it's too late for me? I know it's not. "I have intrinsic value!" I read that in a self-help pamphlet in my gynecologist's waiting room. So I had affairs? So what? I never *loved* Carl, so I was never genuinely unfaithful! Can I stay here?

ARLOC. Of course not.

NESSA. When you say "of course not," you really mean "yes," don't you?

ARLOC. No. You can't. When? For how long?

NESSA. Just a little while, until the settlement settles. I have nowhere else to go! I don't have a cent — one little drink?

ARLOC.   No!

NESSA.   I don't have a credit card! Carl took my name off of them years ago. I charged a Mercedes or something —

ARLOC.   You could go to Aunt Claire.

NESSA.   I HATE HER!!

ARLOC.   She's your sister.

NESSA.   She makes me physically ill. She makes me dizzy. I get light headed and tend towards fainting!

ARLOC.   I thought you liked her —

NESSA.   My God, the woman lives in Nevada! Have you any idea what that sun does to your skin? Claire looks like a bulletin board! And in any event, we haven't spoken in years. You know Uncle Arthur and I had a little — well you know —

ARLOC.   Mother!?

NESSA.   BLAME ME! AS ALWAYS, BLAME ME!! I didn't want it! I wasn't interested. But he cried to me! He wept! You know Claire is frigid — I don't like to criticize, but there you are, there you have it. WHAT AM I GOING TO DO? I have nothing! No money of my own — you should know that all too well. I want to kill myself!

ARLOC.   Don't say that.

NESSA.   God, it's going to be ugly, an ugly divorce. The scenes and the vilification and the lies! The truth alone could freeze your heart.

ARLOC.   What did Carl say when you told him?

NESSA.   Told him what?

ARLOC.   That you're leaving.

NESSA.   Oh ... I didn't *tell* him.

ARLOC.   What!!?

NESSA.   He'd hit me!

ARLOC.   He hits you?! I had no idea!

NESSA.   Not often.

ARLOC.   Still!

NESSA.   Well, never actually. But he would. Now. If I told him. He has a terrible temper! It's those quiet emotional corpses you have to look out for.

ARLOC.   He's never hit you and you haven't told him.

NESSA.   That's right.

ARLOC.   YOU HAVEN'T LEFT HIM AT ALL!

NESSA.   *(Calm, after a pause.)* What are you saying?

ARLOC.   Nothing's happened! Nothing's changed! You just got a little drunk and came over here! You haven't done a thing.

NESSA.   I have! I've turned the corner! While he ate dinner, a fat-free, salt-free, taste-free concoction, covered with brewers yeast, into which I mixed what's left of dear, departed Adelle.

ARLOC.   Oh my God!

NESSA.   Oh, don't be shocked, he'd be happy to have her inside of him if he knew —

ARLOC.   Still.

NESSA.   While he ate dinner, I packed my things. I packed my clothes. And with every pair of slacks my resolve strengthened. Do you understand? I need a little help and you PROMISED me! I'm not a strong person, Arloc. I do things in steps. Baby steps, teeny tiny newborn baby steps. I can't just be all different all at once.

ARLOC.   Well, that's how things happen. All at once.

NESSA.   I'll tell him! I will!

ARLOC.   When?

NESSA.   I'll tell him … tonight.

ARLOC.   *(Going to the door.)* Good. Then I'll believe you.

NESSA.   I'll call him.

ARLOC.   Don't you think you should do this in person?

NESSA.   God no.

ARLOC.   After fourteen years of marriage?

NESSA.   Fifteen years, dear. Fifteen years next month. Trust me.

ARLOC.   Shouldn't you tell him to his face?

NESSA.   Should? Should I? I try not to get involved with shoulds. We live our lives shackled by "shoulds."

ARLOC.   Is that more gynecological wisdom?

NESSA.   That's my own — Obviously, I should. But I can't. I cannot do it. I couldn't look into those sad, needy eyes. His eyes are all liquid and teary and at certain angles seem semi-crossed. I can't tell him face to face. I'll call him!

ARLOC.   Alright. Go ahead. *(Nessa moves to the phone. There*

31

is a long pause.)

NESSA.   You're not going to WATCH me, are you!?... For God's sake.

ARLOC.   Do it!

NESSA.   I'll tell you what. Here's what. You go to my house and get my things. I'll call him while you're gone.

ARLOC.   I can't.

NESSA.   Why not?

ARLOC.   I'm expecting someone.

NESSA.   At this hour? Who is it?

ARLOC.   None of your business.

NESSA.   *(Thrilled.)* Are you dating someone?!

ARLOC.   It's a friend —

NESSA.   I don't believe you.

ARLOC.   I cannot leave!

NESSA.   If someone's coming over, I'll let them in. I'll wait. When you get back I'll go for a walk. I'll go to an all-night movie. You can put me in a hotel if you want. The Plaza, or The Waldorf, but please Arloc, please, not The Park Lane. I hate the Park Lane. Thin towels, thin towels.

ARLOC.   I CAN NOT GO!

NESSA.   You want to see me fail! Don't you? You enjoy feeling superior so you want me to fall on my face! You pretend to take an interest but all the while you're loving my degradation! You keep pushing me to stop drinking, rooting, all the time that I lapse into an alcoholic coma!

ARLOC.   That's not true!

NESSA.   Well, I'm asking for a favor! One tiny, little favor. Is it so much? I don't think it is. I'm your mother. I was there when you were small. I've been there for you — at times! You promised you'd help me!! Please?

ARLOC.   I meant with money —

NESSA.   Oh forget it! I'll just go back to my miserable loveless marriage and wait for old age and premature death to wrap me up in her arms. Just don't visit my grave after I'm gone. I couldn't tolerate the hypocrisy. I will reach up, in death, and kill you! *(She falls to her knees and grovels.)* — Get my bags please! Please, please, please! Please go! Please! I have to get away or I'll kill him in his sleep, or myself! Please fetch them! Please! Please! Please!

ARLOC.   Fine!

NESSA.   *(Cheerful.)* Good, good, good.

ARLOC.   Pull yourself together.

NESSA.   *(Doing so.)* If someone comes, I'll leave.

ARLOC.   Stay right here.

NESSA.   Alright, I'll stay.

ARLOC.   I mean *right* here. In this room.

NESSA.   *(Suspicious.)* Why? What do you mean? What's going on?

ARLOC.   Nothing.

NESSA.   You're lying. I can tell when you're lying. You've got that look on your face you get when you tell me you like me. What's going on here?

ARLOC.   *(Stalling.)* This is very embarrassing.

NESSA.   What were you doing when I arrived?

ARLOC.   Reading.

NESSA.   Naked? You said you weren't dressed. What were you reading?

ARLOC.   I was ... masturbating! Alright? Are you satisfied? I was ... masturbating.

NESSA.   *(After a moment.)* This is so darling.

ARLOC.   I was — masturbating, and — I was using some — stimulus — I cannot believe I have been put in the position of explaining this to my mother.

NESSA.   I feel we're very close now. This is a wonderful Mother/Son/parent/close moment.

ARLOC.   I didn't have time to put it away.

NESSA.   Oh, I don't care about that. What was it? Videos? Blow-up dolls, rubber goods?

ARLOC.   I care! I would find it extremely embarrassing if you were to see it, them, it.

NESSA.   I love you so much at this moment.

ARLOC.   Just stay here.

NESSA.   Fine.

ARLOC.   *(Putting on his coat.)* Thank you. I'll be back in *ten* minutes.

NESSA.   I'll call him right now. It's the two, large Vuitton bags in my big closet. And three hat-boxes on the shelf. And a make-up case. I can't tell you how much I appreciate this!

ARLOC.   God. *(She kisses Arloc. He exits. She pours herself another drink and downs it. With some trepidation, she goes to the phone. She centers herself and becomes quite serious. She lights a cigarette and dials.)*

NESSA.   Carl. It's me ... I'm not going to tell you where I am — I have to talk to you. Carl ... I know things.... I don't want to talk about it.... No.... Listen to me, listen to me, Carl. I'm not coming back. *(A long pause.)* Well, I know you think you do ... I know ... *(She is near tears.)* ... Please don't do this ... don't ... because there's no point ... I've decided ... I have decided. It's done ... *(She starts to weep.)* I'm sorry. I'm sorry — I just ... I'm sorry. Don't make me, don't make me be cruel and say things ... there's no point and the list is too long — *(Suddenly Boyd, still tied to the chair and gagged, comes flying out of the bedroom, knocking the door off it's hinges, having, apparently, hurled himself at it. He lies on the floor, writhing a bit. Nessa stares at him, for a long time, completely startled. Then, with grand composure.)* I'll have to get back to you, Carl. *(She hangs up the phone. She is very embarrassed and doesn't know where to look. Then she decides and crosses, slowly to Boyd, feigning a casual air the whole time.)* Hello.... Hello there ... I'm Nessa, Arloc's mother. *(She extends a hand, out of habit, but retracts it at once, somewhat frightened and adjusts her hair. Boyd writhes and makes unintelligible sounds.)* Are you a friend of Arloc's? *(His answer is a wordless grunt.)* I can't understand you. YOU HAVE FEATHERS IN YOUR MOUTH. *(He makes louder sounds. Nessa looks around.)* Tell me, I hope you don't mind my asking you this, but, why *are* you tied up like that? Do you mind my asking? Is it personal? Is this a "sex-thing?" Is this a game of some sort? Is this some kind of — "gay-homosexual-bondage-carnal-role-playing" thing? *(Boyd is shrieking "UNTIE ME!" but is not understandable.)* I'm really very open-minded. I am. So you needn't be embarrassed ... I've seen films and whatnot. On the television. *We* have cable. I've seen films: men, women, you know, that sort of thing ... IT'S *VERY* NICE MEETING YOU,

34

but I don't think I was supposed to — see you. I don't — Should I put you back? *(Boyd shakes his head, violently. She sits his chair upright and sits, herself, quite casually, as if they were old friends chatting.)* You know Arloc doesn't introduce me to his friends. I assumed he had none. He's very private. I don't think he's happy. You come as a great relief.... Is he happy? Have the two of you been "dating" long? Where did you meet? Not in one of those "bars" I hope. Does he ever talk about me? Would you like a drink? *(Boyd nods wildly. She speaks to herself as she crosses to the bar and pours him a drink.)* I bet you would like a drink. I know I'd like a drink. I had no idea such things went on. Still waters. Still waters. *(To Boyd.)* Scotch alright? *(He nods. She pours the drink and goes to him. She realizes he can't drink it.)* Oh just a minute. *(She gets a letter opener and cuts the rope that holds his gag, and removes it.)*

BOYD.   UNTIE ME!!!!

NESSA.   I don't understand.

BOYD.   UNTIE ME!!

NESSA.   You don't *want* to be tied up?

BOYD.   OF COURSE NOT YOU FUCKING IDIOT!!! NOW UNTIE ME!! RIGHT NOW!!

NESSA.   Please don't shout at me. I've had a very bad evening. I seem to have left my husband. We've had problems, you know. That was him on the phone —

BOYD.   I DON'T CARE!

NESSA.   *(Insulted.)* Well!

BOYD.   YOUR SON IS INSANE! HE'S OUT OF HIS FUCKING MIND!!

NESSA.   I don't think I appreciate —

BOYD.   UN!! TIE!! ME!! NOW!!

NESSA.   I don't know. I don't think I should *interfere*. Really, Arloc and I have, at best, a tenuous relationship. Tonight's been a big step forward and I wouldn't want to meddle.

BOYD.   I'VE BEEN KIDNAPPED! DON'T YOU UNDERSTAND!?

NESSA.   *(Amused.)* Oh, I find that highly unlikely. My son has some strange ideas but I can't believe he's involved in anything criminal.

BOYD.   BELIEVE IT!! HE'S NUTS!

NESSA.   *(Imperious.)* You are a guest in this house.

BOYD.   I AM NOT! HE FORCED ME!! GET THE POLICE! GET THE FUCKING COPS!

NESSA.   I will not. This is my son you're talking about —

BOYD.   I'LL HAVE HIM ARRESTED! I'LL FUCKING KILL HIM!

NESSA.   Just stop shouting please. You're driving nails into my head with your voice.

BOYD.   Please untie me.

NESSA.   Now, when you say he kidnapped you, what exactly do you mean?

BOYD.   I mean he kidnapped me!

NESSA.   Oh. Did he hit you over the head? Did he hold chloroform in front of your nose? He's not particularly prepossessing, physically. How exactly did he "kidnap" you?

BOYD.   He seduced me, sort of.

NESSA.   *(Delighted.)* Really?

BOYD.   We were going to have sex.

NESSA.   And who's idea was that?

BOYD.   HIS!!

NESSA.   *(Cheerful.)* You've had a lovers' spat. Isn't that sweet? It's very healthy I think. The expression of conflict is a healthy sign. I read that in a pamphlet in my gynecologist's waiting room. — I think we should wait for Arloc to return. You can cool off and, trust me, the two of you will work this out.

BOYD.   WE ARE NOT LOVERS! I met him TODAY!

NESSA.   *(Ignoring this.)* Relationships have ups and downs: rough/smooth, rough/smooth. You know. What matters is: Do you love him?

BOYD.   OF COURSE NOT! He is completely crazy!

NESSA.   *(Knowing better.)* So why are you here? And, why exactly are you dressed like that?

BOYD.   I'm an angel!

NESSA.   *(After a long moment.)* And Arloc is crazy?

BOYD.   AT RADIO CITY!! In the Christmas show! I herald the arrival of the birth of Jesus! Arloc came backstage and flirted with me. He was obviously infatuated. I didn't encourage him! I felt sorry for him!

NESSA.   *(Suspicious.)* Did you know who he is?

BOYD.   What does that mean?

NESSA.   Did you recognize him?

BOYD.   From *what?*

NESSA.   My son has been in the papers. His face has been in the news.

BOYD.   Who is he?

NESSA.   Arloc was made very wealthy, very young. You didn't know that?

BOYD.   I felt sorry for him! I came here and he seduced me. I didn't want to be tied up! He offered me money! I don't normally accept money! That isn't how I live! But, I felt sorry him — He tied me up and gagged me. Then he told me that he loved me! Do you understand? He needs help. We spoke today for the first time and he told me he loved me. Now please, please, untie me! *(There is a pause. The truth of what he is saying finally becomes apparent to Nessa. The grim reality has sobered her completely. She sits.)*

NESSA.   I see.

BOYD.   He doesn't know me, how could he love me?!

NESSA.   *(Cruel.)* How *else* could he love you?

BOYD.   He told me I couldn't leave. He told me he would keep me here, that I would fall in love with him — if I stayed. That all he needed was a chance!

NESSA.   *(Moved by this.)* Oh.

BOYD.   NOW PLEASE! CUT THIS! THIS HURTS!

NESSA.   *(A little fearful.)* You'll call the police.

BOYD.   No! No! I won't I swear it! Just untie me.

NESSA.   You won't tell anyone?

BOYD.   Never. I won't. I promise.

NESSA.   Why should I trust you?

BOYD.   I was going to rob him! Look! Look in my coat.

NESSA.   This?

BOYD.   Look! There's a paperweight — *(Nessa reaches into the coat pocket and pulls out the paperweight. She holds it, studying it, as he continues.)* — he told me it was crystal, I assumed it was worth something and I was going to steal it! I won't call the police. If I do you can tell them I was going to rob him. I swear. Please ... now, please untie me. *(Nessa holds the paperweight in her hand and thinks a moment. Then without speaking. She replaces it on the bar. She takes the letter opener and is about to cut him free, then thinks better of it.)*

NESSA. *(Softly.)* Stay.

BOYD. What?

NESSA. I'm asking you to stay.

BOYD. No. Absolutely not.

NESSA. Give him what he wants. Give him a chance.

BOYD. There is no chance —

NESSA. There's always a chance ... that you could. Try. Stay with him.

BOYD. No!

NESSA. It must mean a lot to him. You must.

BOYD. I don't care!

NESSA. He loves you.

BOYD. Just let me go — I won't tell anyone. I swear to God!

NESSA. I don't think Arloc's ever loved someone, really,

BOYD. Please!

NESSA. — who loved him.

BOYD. This isn't love! It's a sick obsession.

NESSA. Whatever it is, it could be —

BOYD. Never.

NESSA. If you taught him, showed him. If *you* loved *him.*

BOYD. But I don't!

NESSA. You could try. You could pretend. It's not that hard.

BOYD. Why should I?

NESSA. I'll pay you. You were willing to have sex for money. I'm asking you to love him for more.

BOYD. Fuck you!

NESSA. What could you have?

BOYD. Plenty.

NESSA. What do you need?

BOYD. Nothing.

NESSA. Tell me how much.

BOYD. I'm not a fucking whore!

NESSA. Of course not.

BOYD.   Get him a fucking whore.

NESSA.   *(Begging now.)* He wants you and I want him to have you. I'll pay you very well. I need to help him. Please stay.

BOYD.   No. *(She removes her necklace.)*

NESSA.   Here. I'll give you this.

BOYD.   Fake pearls?

NESSA.   Real pearls. This necklace was a gift from my first father-in-law — after an "assignation." And it's all I have, but I'll give it to you. It's worth, I'd guess, many, thousands of dollars. But all of it. You need to have a perfect set, perfectly matched in size and color. Think what you could do with thirty thousand dollars, maybe forty. It's the only thing I own of value. I'll give it to you, and you give yourself to him. Let him think you love him. Make love to him. *(She smiles ruefully, looking at the necklace.)* I've done a terrible thing and I want to make it right. I'll give it to you one pearl at a time, every day. Each day. Every day you love him. *(The act curtain closes and a pool of light comes up on Arloc as he was at the beginning of the play. He is calmer.)*

ARLOC.   Fine. Judge me if you want. I took something, some-*one* against his will. But I wasn't me. I don't know who I was. When I was younger, I wanted to be an actor on the stage. I was in plays in school. I was in *The Cherry Orchard.* I was in *Long Day's Journey Into Night.* And I loved being someone else. Even Mary Tyrone, poor, lonely, drug addicted, Mary Tyrone. The day he came I found a spot, dark on my skin, the size of a quarter. And in my home, on a table, beneath a paper-weight, there sits an envelope that I cannot bring myself to open. I'd like nothing more than to be someone else. Almost anyone else. Once I was on the stage, in someone else's clothes, speaking someone else's words, with someone else's hope. And I was so happy … *(He smiles.)* for a time. *(Black-out.)*

END OF ACT ONE

ACT TWO

"The New Year"

Scene 1

Nessa walks into a pool of light. She is wearing a rather elegant peignoir. She addresses the audience.

NESSA. And so we found ourselves together. *(A light comes up on Arloc.)*

ARLOC. I came back home and they were "chatting."

NESSA. That first night was ... difficult. The idea that I was leaving Carl *was* liberating but, I must admit, completely frightening.

ARLOC. I was bleeding when I walked in the door.

NESSA. The fact is, I'd never been on my own — granted, I wasn't really on my own now.

ARLOC. I was bleeding from my mouth and they assumed that Carl had hit me, but he hadn't. He shouted and begged but he never touched me.

NESSA. What was really bothering me, aside from a splitting headache, brought on, no doubt, from drinking *gallons* of various fermented beverages, was Arloc.

ARLOC. Yet blood was flowing from my mouth. I may have bitten myself or cut my tongue, but I decided, don't laugh, that it was a sign. That I was somehow close to God and that I had had some sort of "dental stigmata." *(Arloc's light goes out.)*

NESSA. I realized that what I had thought were isolated incidents were more than that. I found myself, in the middle of the night, unable to sleep. *(The lights come up, suggesting the middle of the night. She sits and stares at the Matisse and starts to cry. After a moment, Boyd enters. He wears pajama bottoms.)*

BOYD. What are you doing?

NESSA. Nothing.

BOYD. Are you crying?

NESSA. No.

BOYD. I thought I heard you.

NESSA. How's Arloc?

BOYD. The bleeding's stopped.

NESSA. Thank God. Only Arloc could interpret periodontal disease as divine intervention.

BOYD. Why are you up?

NESSA. I was just looking at this. I couldn't sleep.

BOYD. Oh?

NESSA. My head aches.

BOYD. You shouldn't drink so much.

NESSA. I'm not drinking. Everyone picks on me. I'm not drinking *now*. Alright?

BOYD. Good.

NESSA. *(After a moment.)* There's nothing left.

BOYD. You drank it all?

NESSA. Yes ... I was thinking. Do you know the story behind this — thing, this work of art?

BOYD. No.

NESSA. God knows how much it cost. Probably more than I can imagine. Not that it matters to Arloc, but, you know, money, money, money. He was seeing this boy, man, boy-man. I don't know how old he was. But he was absolutely *rhapsodic* about him. Really just head over heels. Whenever I called him on the phone it was Anthony this and Anthony that — a little sickening really, but I was happy for him. To find someone, you know. We went shopping for this — Matisse together. We got along better then. When I say "then," I mean that week. That was a good week. We were friends that week. So I went with him to dealers and auctions. He was going to give it to Anthony as a gift, when he moved in. Arloc told me they planned to live together. Naturally, I wanted to meet him and naturally, Arloc was very reluctant, always embarrassed by me, I think. The way children are of their mothers. But I pressed him. So he arranged a lunch at The Café Des Artiste. Do you know it?

BOYD. No.

NESSA. It's very nice. They have a very good wine list. Lunch was scheduled for two. I was careful. I was nervous. I drank water. Two o'clock arrived: Arloc and I waited. At two thirty we ordered. At quarter to three we panicked, and Arloc made a series of phone calls and sad attempts at feeble excuses. At three fifteen a very good-looking young man rushed into the restaurant. He walked, very angry and very quickly to our table. He didn't sit down. He stood there and said — I remember it like yesterday — he said, "Are you Arloc's mother? I'm Anthony." He said, "Listen, I wasn't going to come at all, but I thought we should talk, because I don't know what else to do. I've tried everything." Arloc was breathing very deeply. "I *have* tried everything. I don't know what Arloc told you, but let me be very clear. Your son and I had a couple of dates. They were fine, but I'm seeing someone else. I was when we met and I'm going to continue. Now, I was wrong to start and I admit that. But Arloc ... he will *not* leave me alone! He won't stop — I'm sorry — bothering me! I've tried everything. Now I've come here. So please talk to him! Talk to your son!" ... And then he left.

BOYD. I'm sorry.

NESSA. We never talked about it. But we don't talk about much. He paid the check in silence.... He falls in love, it seems, repeatedly, with the wrong people.

BOYD. Oh?

NESSA. People who don't care. *(She holds back tears.)* And *I* think, I *believe*, that it's my fault.

BOYD. What does that mean?

NESSA. He doesn't really want someone — to care about him.

BOYD. I don't understand.

NESSA. He doesn't think he deserves it.

BOYD. Oh.

NESSA. And that's my fault.

BOYD. It's not.

NESSA. When Arloc was five, we, his father and I, noticed

he was ... strange.

BOYD.   In what way?

NESSA.   He cried too much. He didn't eat. And we, Arloc's father and I, took him for psychological testing. He was five. And they told us, Arloc's father and me, that we should put him into therapy. To cure him.

BOYD.   Of what?

NESSA.   Being gay.

BOYD.   Cure him?

NESSA.   And we did just that. He was five. We didn't know a thing.... We accomplished nothing, of course. But Arloc managed to fool everyone until his father died and I think about it all the time. His face as he walked down the hall. I didn't want to do it. *(She's crying now.)*

BOYD.   Don't cry.

NESSA.   I'm not stupid —

BOYD.   Please. Let me help you. Let me. Give yourself to me. I'll help you. *(Boyd takes her head in his hands and kisses her. It is gentle at first, but becomes passionate. After a moment, he steps away.)* Wait. *(He shuts the bedroom door. The light diminishes, leaving only Nessa lighted.)*

NESSA.   He shut the door so Arloc wouldn't hear us. And we made love. And I felt terrible and I was twenty years old with all of my mistakes ahead of me. And it was ... *fantastic!*... Well, you know. *(Blackout.)*

Scene 2

Three weeks later. The lights come up on Arloc's living room. It is somewhat messier than it was previously. The telephone rings. From the bedroom, offstage, we hear the voices of Arloc and Boyd.

BOYD.   *(Offstage.)* Arloc, please!

ARLOC.   *(Offstage.)* No.

BOYD.   *(Offstage.)* I'm begging!

ARLOC. *(Offstage.)* Let go of me.

BOYD. *(Offstage.)* Where are you going? *(The phone rings.)*

ARLOC. *(Offstage.)* To answer the phone. *(Arloc enters from the bedroom, dressed casually.)*

BOYD. *(Offstage.)* Arloc!

ARLOC. *(Into the phone.)* Hello?... Oh, Hello, Carl.... She's not here.... Out.... Out. I don't know.... Doing errands ...

BOYD. *(Offstage.)* I miss you!

ARLOC. Yes, I told her ... I told her you called.... Yesterday.... And the day before and the day before and the day before! And the day before that! You've called every day, Carl, for three weeks! Every day, every hour, every fifteen minutes on weekends! And I have told her, I have relayed that information to her on every occasion! *(Boyd enters wearing a silk bathrobe, clearly very expensive. Boyd circles Arloc, filming him with a video camera. Arloc, into phone.)* My guess? My guess is she doesn't want to talk to you — Please, Carl it's degrading when you cry.... Degrading for me.... Well, yes. I suppose it is more degrading for you ... I'll tell her Carl. Yes, red meat. I will. Good-bye, Carl. *(He hangs up the phone.)* That was Carl.

BOYD. Again?

ARLOC. He says he's sick. He says he's killing himself.

BOYD. Pills?

ARLOC. Red meat.

BOYD. Slow but steady.

ARLOC. He's losing his mind — Stop that.

BOYD. Can I say one thing?

ARLOC. He's completely obsessed.

BOYD. The camera loves you.

ARLOC. Put that down.

BOYD. You're going to be spectacular.

ARLOC. I haven't said I'd do it.

BOYD. You'll do it.

ARLOC. Don't push me.

BOYD. You have to! A return to your element! We'll capture your greatest work on film!

ARLOC. It was *many* years ago and I never said — I doubt that I was very good! I was fourteen!

BOYD. "Arloc Simpson is Mary Tyrone!"

ARLOC. Have you been playing with your dosage?

BOYD. It'll be a triumph!

ARLOC. A film with one actor?

BOYD. Daring in its simplicity.

ARLOC. I should never've given you my copy.

BOYD. Shocking in it's density!

ARLOC. Put that down! — There is no way to make a film of *Long Day's Journey Into Night* with ONE actor!

BOYD. Voice-overs!

ARLOC. Oh God.

BOYD. All the other parts are voice-overs. The camera stays on you the whole time.

ARLOC. And the scenes I'm not in?

BOYD. We stay on you — sleeping, shooting up. Wondering around the house, slowly succumbing to your morphine addictive madness!

ARLOC. A bad idea gone wrong.

BOYD. We *hear* the scenes from another part of the set.

ARLOC. It's insipid.

BOYD. *(Circling Arloc.)* You'll be brilliant! I see awards in your future, gold statues on the mantel and citations from Cannes! You've waited your whole life to be Mary Tyrone — you understand her! You are her! You have tragedy in your veins and I can capture that and give you immortality!

ARLOC. I'd prefer a tie.

BOYD. Look at me.

ARLOC. PUT IT DOWN! *(Boyd does so. There is a pause. The phone rings. Arloc picks it up. Into phone.)* Hello?... No, Carl! She's not here.... PLEASE stop calling! I can't answer the phone every twenty seconds! *(He hangs up the phone.)*

BOYD. *(Serious, direct.)* Sleep with me.

ARLOC. No.

BOYD. Fuck me.

ARLOC. NO!

BOYD. Then let me —

ARLOC. No! Must every human emotion be expressed physically? Must every encounter between two human beings lead to one inevitable end: sex?

BOYD. Or violence —

ARLOC. Is it impossible for gay men to express mutual affection in any way aside from fucking each other and sucking each other. What about other values!?

BOYD. Values, shmalues! Let's have sex!

ARLOC. I'm not feeling very well.

BOYD. When I came here, you said you wanted a chance. Now *I* want a chance —

ARLOC. I believe I've eaten something spoiled.

BOYD. I want you.

ARLOC. What did I eat today?

BOYD. I need you!

ARLOC. Bad milk. Bad eggs. Bad lunch.

BOYD. Is it me?

ARLOC. Of course not —

BOYD. It is me isn't it? There's something wrong with me! You hate me!

ARLOC. I don't —

BOYD. You hate my hair! Or my voice! You hate my robe!

ARLOC. It's my robe.

BOYD. You don't find me attractive!

ARLOC. I do — You should be happy! Everyone wants to have sex with you! I just want to be with you! (*Phone rings. He answers it. Into the phone.*) Carl! Listen to me —

BOYD. (*Tugging at Arloc.*) Trust me, Arloc. I want to love you. I want to help you.

ARLOC. (*Into the phone.*) I'm sorry — (*To Boyd.*) — it's for you.

BOYD. What? Oh. (*He takes the phone.*) Hello? (*Nessa enters. Under her coat she is wears a denim shirt and jeans. She looks altogether younger and is in very good spirits. She carries a bag of magazines.*)

NESSA. Arloc! I have the most wonderful things to show you!

ARLOC. Where've you been?

NESSA. Out. Working. It's a beautiful day! Have you been in here all morning? The air is a tonic! Winter birds are singing Christmas carols! Everywhere you look the miracle of Christ and modern crass commercialism scalds the eye!

BOYD. *(Into the phone.)* Where is it?

ARLOC. Carl called.

NESSA. Again?

ARLOC. And again, and again. I barely recognize his voice. He has emotions.

NESSA. The poor thing is despondent to the point of farce! I believe he's following me. I mean it! I haven't seen him, but I feel his hot damp breath on the back of my neck at red lights.

BOYD. *(Into the phone.)* What time?

ARLOC. He says he wants to die. He says he's eating sugar. He's eating red meat. He says he's sick.

NESSA. *(Lighting a cigarette.)* Sick? I wonder if Adelle's still repeating on him.

ARLOC. He says he's destroyed.

NESSA. You know what they say. You can't keep a good woman down.

ARLOC. I thought you were giving that up? You told me you quit!

NESSA. Please, darling —

BOYD. *(Into the phone.)* Should we bring anything?

NESSA. I've given up liquor. Isn't that enough? I haven't had a drink in two years!

ARLOC. Three weeks.

NESSA. Do we live in a parallel universe? Is that it? Have I stumbled into a hole in the arbitrary construct of time?

ARLOC. You promised.

NESSA. I *have* to smoke! I do! Honestly. My mouth doesn't know what to do without vodka swimming through it twenty-four hours a day! It was mother's milk to me.

BOYD. *(Into the phone.)* I'll ask. Thanks. *(He hangs up the phone.)*

NESSA. I can't give everything up all at once! — Hello, Boyd. I like your robe — I'm not a, a, a nun for God's sake!

ARLOC. God knows.

NESSA. Isn't it enough that I've eschewed the grape and the grain? I *never* thought I'd make it this long without alcohol! I can't go cold turkey on vice. Baby steps. Baby steps.

BOYD. Does anyone want to go to a party tomorrow night?

ARLOC.   I don't know.

NESSA.   Of course we do! What a stick in the mud! It's New Year's Eve —

BOYD.   Good.

NESSA.   And I'm drinking, Arloc. On *New Year's Eve,* I'm drinking, so don't argue about it. You look at me like Lee Remick in *Wine and Roses.* Honestly! Alright, alright. If it bothers you that much I won't drink. Happy? Are you? Fine. I'll mope around all gloomy and depressed and feeling left out and sorry for myself, dry as a bone on New Year's Eve. — Please! Please! Please! Just champagne! That's all. Champagne, which, if you ask me, isn't *real* alcohol anyway. It's bad 7-up.

ARLOC.   Whose party?

BOYD.   The toy soldiers'. They are having a New Year's party on Jose's roof.

NESSA.   Fabulous!

ARLOC.   I'm afraid of heights.

NESSA.   What should I wear? Black? Fur? What?

BOYD.   You are?

ARLOC.   Yes.

NESSA.   Is it dressy?

BOYD.   *(Shaking his head.)* They're toys.

NESSA.   Arloc will come. Won't you, Arloc? If the height bothers you you can lie on your stomach. I understand that helps.

ARLOC.   *(Annoyed.)* Mother, what do you mean, you've been working?

NESSA.   Pardon?

ARLOC.   Working on what?

NESSA.   *(As if Arloc's insane.)* The set.

ARLOC.   What?

NESSA.   We discussed it! We did! I have witnesses — well one witness. You said I could redecorate — and Boyd said that would be wonderful because we could use a new set — for the film —

ARLOC.   I said you could buy sheets!

NESSA.   Well. I interpreted that as a vote of confidence. Wait till you see! I'm a genius! I have wonderful things to show you!

48

(Boyd "films" Nessa and Arloc, moving around them.)

BOYD.   If you're really worried about carrying the whole film, Arloc, Nessa can be in it with you.

NESSA.   Could I!? Really? Who'll I play?

BOYD.   James Tyrone.

NESSA.   Who does Arloc play?

BOYD.   Mary Tyrone.

NESSA.   I adore the avant garde!!

ARLOC.   The whole project lacks dignity.

NESSA.   Now, Boyd, you'll have to film me through gauze, or cheese cloth. I don't work after six P.M. or before nine. And rewrite all you want but I have approval of the final draft —

ARLOC.   *(Losing patience.)* What's in the bag?

NESSA.   Sensational things! Let me show you. *(She pulls out magazines and swatches.)*

BOYD.   This'll be great!

NESSA.   Arloc, switch places. He's getting my bad side.

ARLOC.   There's no film!!

NESSA.   I should still look my best. *(She switches places with Arloc.)* Here, dear. Look at these. And these. *(The phone rings. Boyd goes to it.)*

ARLOC.   You want to turn my home into a Turkish bordello?

NESSA.   Oh loosen up! For heaven's sake. This is very chic! Today!

BOYD.   *(Into the phone.)* Hello?

NESSA.   Newsy!

BOYD.   *(Into the phone.)* Oh hello.

NESSA.   Everyone's doing *Harem* this year. You know Marrakech and mats, straw thatching and mosquito nets. And geckos! Geckos everywhere!

BOYD.   It's Carl.

ARLOC.   *Long Days Journey Into Night* is set in Connecticut!

NESSA.   I'm not here — And Mary Tyrone was a woman. What's your point?

ARLOC.   It's hideous.

BOYD.   *(Into the phone.)* I'll tell her. *(He hangs up the phone, and resumes "filming" them.)*

NESSA.   Hideous is a strong word, Arloc. A very strong word.

BOYD.   He's eating chocolate. *(He resumes filming them.)*

NESSA.   Who cares? — Fine. Fine, fine. You don't like Harem. How about this?

ARLOC.   *(Disdainful.)* What is it?

NESSA.   Furniture.

ARLOC.   It is?

NESSA.   This is very lively! This is tomorrow!

BOYD.   I think it's great.

NESSA.   It's the day after!

ARLOC.   It's furniture?

NESSA.   It's blow-up furniture!

BOYD.   You two'll be brilliant together.

ARLOC.   It looks like the sixties.

NESSA.   Well it *is* the sixties, you know. The nineties *are* the sixties. The eighties were the fifties. The seventies were the forties. The sixties ... were, just, well, they were, you know, themselves. Ugly at the time, I'll tell you that.

ARLOC.   Exactly my point.

NESSA.   But we've refined them. It's ugly now, but refined in a different kind of a sort of a way.

ARLOC.   I said you could buy sheets!

NESSA.   You are so narrow.

ARLOC.   I said you could buy shelf-paper!

NESSA.   CAN'T YOU EVER BE ENTHUSIASTIC ABOUT THINGS! I mean this could be a tremendous amount of fun. This decorating thing! I think I've found my niche! And this room needs more than a face lift — this room needs a lyposuction and a chemical peel. Look around, Arloc. Look around — Boyd, would you get me a glass of juice? *(Boyd exits.)* LOOK AROUND! GOD! You don't like Harem and you don't like blow-up. I suppose there's no point in showing you the living sponge dinette! Is there? No, no. No, you just want to live in the goddamn FRICK MUSEUM! Well I guess I'm wasting my time trying to resuscitate you AND this apartment. Call the wreckers. Let's just tear it down and live in a TAR-PAPER HUT ON FIFTH AVENUE.

BOYD.   *(Re-entering.)* We're out of juice.

NESSA.   *(Collapsing.)* My health regime! I'm going to die! I'll

50

perish right here in this room! This dreary, dull, oppressive, OUT-OF-DATE, OUT-OF-STYLE, OUT-OF-TOUCH *WAX MUSEUM* ROOM!

ARLOC. *(Flat.)* Would you like me to get you some?

NESSA. Would you? Would you really do that for me? Just for me? I can't thank you enough.

ARLOC. *(Getting his coat.)* We wouldn't want you to die. Would we?

NESSA. I adore you! Go to the good store. Not the one on the corner. The good one, with the exotics. Get a couple of bottles, alright? A few bottles of that — what it is — mung bean or kiwi or whatever it is.

ARLOC. I'll be right back. *(He exits.)*

NESSA. *(Calling after him.)* It's a colonic!

BOYD. I can't go on.

NESSA. Please don't start on me Boyd. I've told you, no. No, no, no. We cannot sleep together. I can't continue. I'm putting it in the past. As of this minute we're a memory.

BOYD. That's not it.

NESSA. *(Not hearing him.)* I know it's hard for you. It's hard for me too. Looking at you every day. Wanting you inside of me. Looking at you, looking at me. Your skin, your hands, your lips — Jesus Christ.

BOYD. Listen, Nessa —

NESSA. But I feel so duplicitous! I'm a horrible human being and I don't deserve you. Why aren't you dressed? You look unbelievable. My God. Are you tan in December? HOLD ME!! *(She wraps her arms around him.)*

BOYD. He won't sleep with me.

NESSA. What's wrong with him? *(The phone rings. She gestures that he should answer it. He does so.)*

BOYD. *(Into the phone.)* Hello?... Oh, hello Carl. *(Nessa kisses his neck over and over while he talks on the phone. Into phone.)* She's not here.... I'll tell her you called. *(He hangs up the phone. She continues kissing him.)*

NESSA. You taste fantastic!

BOYD. I can't go on like this.

NESSA. You taste like heaven.

BOYD. I've tried everything!

NESSA. You taste like God!

BOYD. Stop it!! *(Nessa stops. There is a pause.)*

NESSA. Maybe it's me.

BOYD. What do you mean?

NESSA. The problem with Arloc.... Maybe it's my presence. Maybe it intimidates him. You know mother/child, mother/child.

BOYD. I don't think so.

NESSA. I should leave. I should go somewhere else.

BOYD. Don't.

NESSA. I can afford it now. I stole some of Arloc's credit cards.

BOYD. If you go, I'll tell him everything. That you've been paying me.

NESSA. You wouldn't do that.

BOYD. I wouldn't want to, but —

NESSA. Alright, alright! Well then, do you think it's physical? Do you think it's medical? Maybe he can't, actually, get, well, you know, you know.

BOYD. It's not. He can. We've done everything but.

NESSA. Really?

BOYD. We've kissed and held and touched each other. We've told each other we *loved* each other! I've felt him against me. And at night in his sleep — and I don't understand it! I thought he was in love in with me! I want him! I want him to need me. He has to accept me and I don't understand. This is no neurosis — this is a tangible fear — I thought — It's not working! I thought he *loved* me!!... I thought he did!! *(Abruptly the lighting diminishes leaving only Nessa in light. She addresses the audience.)*

NESSA. And then it struck me. All at once. I understood suddenly. And I couldn't see a thing. *(A second pool of light comes up on Arloc, who addresses the audience.)*

ARLOC. It was the happiest month of my life.

NESSA. I seemed to come out of my body. I was watching myself in a room with Boyd. But I couldn't hear what we were saying.

ARLOC.   It was paradise really. We were living in a miracle.

NESSA.   We were in a silent film.

ARLOC.   And I noticed, on my skin, the spot looked paler.

NESSA.   The noise was in my head.

ARLOC.   The only thing that marred my bliss was that I couldn't touch him. I couldn't love him the way I wanted to. I couldn't risk it. Hurting him.

NESSA.   I understood and I was going to be sick.

ARLOC.   There are precautions one can take, but I was too afraid to explore them.

NESSA.   Right there. At that moment.

ARLOC.   I still didn't know of course. The envelope from the hospital sat, still, unopened on the table, taunting me every day: "You think you're happy? Do you? It can end like that! All over like that!"

NESSA.   I was shaking. God. No. Don't let it be true. Why didn't he tell me?

ARLOC.   I CAN KILL YOU, LIKE THAT!

NESSA.   Why should he? Who am I to him?

ARLOC.   I tried not to think about it. I couldn't let it go. And I couldn't face it.

NESSA.   It hit me all at once. I understood *everything*.

ARLOC.   I tried to pretend it wasn't there.

NESSA.   I understood the horrible, monster-ugly world.

ARLOC.   I dreamed and prayed and walked and shopped. I took my secret with me. I went to Tiffany's, and bought presents. I went to sleep with my secret.

NESSA.   I understood my son was positive. I understood my son was sick.

ARLOC.   There had begun a change in my body. The atoms of my flesh vibrate faster and they hum a sound I hear in my head.

NESSA.   All at once.

ARLOC.   The sound is pure and I am no longer me.

NESSA.   I want to die.

ARLOC.   I am something else. I am not human. (*His light goes out.*)

NESSA.   Don't die. (*Blackout.*)

Scene 3

The next evening. We see through the window that it is snowing. Carl is pacing, talking to Arloc.

Carl wears a business suit, his coat is on a chair. Arloc is dressed for a party. They are civil with each other, but there is a tension in the room, residue from years of animosity. Sitting in a corner, on the floor are shopping bags from an audio-visual store.

CARL.   Thank you for letting me in. It's freezing out there, snowing again. I was losing the feeling in my fingers. I was about to burn money in a smudge-pot for warmth. My life was flashing in front of my eyes and it was a terrible movie with a sad, sad end. I appreciate your letting me in. I know the last time we had that little misunderstanding and I apologize. I shouldn't have raised my voice, but I was out of my mind. You understand? You were walking away with her things. You were taking my *life* away in two suitcases. What was I supposed to do? I *don't* understand her. She won't communicate. She won't talk to me. She hung up on me three weeks ago and I haven't spoken to her since. I haven't been to work, you know. I haven't been to bed. I can't concentrate on anything.

ARLOC.   You can't stay, Carl.

CARL.   That night, the night you came and took her things, I took a knife and tried to cut myself. That surprises you, doesn't it? Well, I wasn't thinking. I watched myself press the blade to the skin on my wrist, but my hands were shaking and I couldn't grip the handle. It's simply not fair! I'm a human being and I deserve more.

ARLOC.   Should I call you a taxi?

CARL.   You see, we were happy. We were. We had our problems. What couple doesn't? But we were happy. We enjoyed our friends. We enjoyed each other. We traveled and shared things, and I was happy just watching her. Watching TV ... I

54

was happy.

ARLOC.   I think you should go.

CARL.   She loves me! I know she does. She doesn't show it.
Fine. That's who she is. She never asks me how I am. She
never asks me how I feel. But that doesn't mean a thing.
Adelle used to ask me, "What*ever* is wrong with you?" She
never said "what's wrong with you?" She said, "What*ever* is
wrong with you?" It was an affectation and frankly irritating.

ARLOC.   I don't know if you heard me —

CARL.   It's not fair! What do I have!? I have two children,
who call me when they want something, when they need
money. I have a boy and a girl who hate me, who think I
didn't love their mother. But when Adelle died, I wished it
was me. And then I met your Nessa. And I was glad I'd lived.

ARLOC.   She doesn't want to see you.

CARL.   I assumed she was fine. I assumed everything was fine.
Does she talk to you? Does she confide in you? I shouldn't
put you in that position. It's not right, really. I'm sorry. Forget I asked. Has she told you what she's thinking? I'm sorry,
I shouldn't pressure you. Has she? Excuse me, really. I'll just
wait for your mother. I'll talk to her. Has she? I'm sorry. Well?

ARLOC.   She *won't* see you, Carl.

CARL.   Of course she will. There are codes of conduct, civi-
lized patterns of behavior — I'll wait.

ARLOC.   You'll wait?

CARL.   I stared at the knife as if it were someone else's wrist.
It was a grapefruit knife, very flimsy. I don't know that it would
do much damage and I don't know why we have them. I don't
care for grapefruit.

ARLOC.   It's New Years Eve. Aren't you going somewhere?

CARL.   The house is filled with knives and I don't know
where they come from.

ARLOC.   To a party or something?

CARL.   No.

ARLOC.   Don't you have plans?

CARL.   No.

ARLOC.   You're not doing *anything?*

CARL.   No. Nothing! No.

ARLOC. *(Mumbles to himself.)* Sort of pathetic, really.

CARL. What?

ARLOC. *(Clearly.)* I said that's sort of pathetic.

CARL. Oh. *(Pause.)* Who would I go with besides my wife?

ARLOC. *(Ironic.)* Hookers?

CARL. *(Referring to the bags.)* What's all that?

ARLOC. We're making a movie.

CARL. We?

ARLOC. Mother and Boyd and I..

CARL. I see …

ARLOC. It's sort of an experiment.

CARL. Oh…. Can I be in it?

ARLOC. Pardon me?

CARL. Is there a part for me?

ARLOC. You want to be in it?

CARL. I think so, yes. What's it about? It doesn't matter. What's the plot? I want to be in it.

ARLOC. I don't think so.

CARL. But you'll think about it?

ARLOC. No.

CARL. I think it's a good idea.

ARLOC. Why?

CARL. We could spend some time together.

ARLOC. You and I?

CARL. Nessa and I!

ARLOC. Oh.

CARL. — If she refuses to come home. So, can I be in it?

ARLOC. No.

CARL. I don't have to have a big part.

ARLOC. I'm afraid not.

CARL. Don't reject me out of hand! I'll audition! I'll test! I might be better than you think. I might be very, very good.

ARLOC. You can't be in it!

CARL. I'm just asking for a chance! I don't think that's un-reasonable. I think *you're* unreasonable! I don't need a good part! I'll take a walk-on or something small, maybe something in the end? One good scene! What do you think?

ARLOC. I can't be any clearer!

CARL. Fine! It doesn't hurt to ask. *(Arloc goes to the door.)*
ARLOC. I'll have her call you. I don't have any idea when she'll be back — it could be late. I don't know where she is.
CARL. *(Sitting.)* I don't care.
ARLOC. I don't know when to expect her.
CARL. I said, I'll wait.
ARLOC. *(Returning.)* Well, fine. But if she wanted to talk to you, she'd have answered your calls. Don't you think?
CARL. She doesn't know what she *wants*! She's drunk half the time.
ARLOC. Not anymore.
CARL. What do you mean?
ARLOC. She hasn't had a drink in weeks.
CARL. Nessa?
ARLOC. Not a sip.
CARL. She must be very unhappy.
ARLOC. She's been sober since she got here.
CARL. Has she had a breakdown of some kind!?
ARLOC. She's on a health regime.
CARL. My God, she's fallen apart.
ARLOC. She's doing very well.
CARL. She's masking her sorrow, over-reacting in a pathological, self-destructive manner: Not drinking!
ARLOC. She doesn't *want* to drink. She doesn't want to see you. And she doesn't want to leave.
CARL. *(He has an idea.)* What do *you* want?
ARLOC. What do you mean?
CARL. Don't you want her out of here? She must be in the way.
ARLOC. Not particularly.
CARL. You could ask her.
ARLOC. What?
CARL. You could ask her to go. Tell her she's intruding. Say you need your privacy.
ARLOC. I *don't* need my privacy.
CARL. You could lie! If you ask her to leave, she'll have no place to go. She'll *have* come home.
ARLOC. You want me to throw my mother into the street?

CARL. Yes!

ARLOC. What kind of sub-human do you take me for?

CARL. I'll pay you!

ARLOC. I don't need your money.

CARL. *(Taking out a checkbook.)* How much? I'll write a check!

ARLOC. Put that away!

CARL. Name a figure.

ARLOC. She's my mother! I'm not going to sell her!

CARL. You should be thinking about what's best for her, Arloc. I know you don't care for me — You've never liked me and I don't know why. But whatever animosity you feel ought to be put to one side. You ought to consider your mother now.

ARLOC. I am!

CARL. I'm not so horrible. Really. I give to charity. I'm nice to animals. People like me! Some people.

ARLOC. Who?

CARL. I'm a human being and I'm in trouble! If I was a stranger, lying in the street, bleeding, begging, asking for help, you'd help! I'm begging! Tell her to come home!

ARLOC. No.

CARL. Tell her I love her. Tell her I need her! I need her! One of these nights I'm going to grab a knife with possibilities!

ARLOC. Carl —

CARL. *(Turning away.)* This is very uncomfortable for me! I'm not used to this. I've been very attached to the idea of my dignity. This is strange to me, this display of — feelings.

ARLOC. I can't say it becomes you.

CARL. *(Absolutely not crying.)* I'm crying, aren't I?

ARLOC. No.

CARL. Look closely.

ARLOC. No, nothing.

CARL. I can feel it.

ARLOC. You're not crying.

CARL. This is very upsetting. I want to be in control! I don't want to cry!

ARLOC. You're not crying.

CARL. I know when I'm crying!!! I know when tears are

streaming down my face! When I'm falling apart! When I've been reduced to a weak, pathetic sobbing mass of protoplasm.

ARLOC. You are absolutely NOT crying.

CARL. I'm *sobbing.*

ARLOC. I've never seen anyone not-crying more.

CARL. This is terrible. I didn't want this to happen.

ARLOC. What? Not-crying?

CARL. I don't want her to see me like this.

ARLOC. You're right. Maybe you should go.

CARL. I have to pull myself together.

ARLOC. From what?

CARL. I'm going to the bathroom, Arloc. When I come out, I'll be completely composed. *(Carl exits into the bathroom. We hear him moan very loudly. "Aaaaahhhh." Nessa and Boyd burst into the room. Under their coats, she is dressed for a party, he wears his angel costume without the wings. They each carry a bottle of champagne — Boyd has drunk most of his.)*

BOYD. Merry Christmas!   NESSA. Happy New Year!

NESSA. That was last week! My God, what's wrong with you? Everyone knows Christmas was last week.

BOYD. I'm sorry.

ARLOC. Christ. You're drunk.

NESSA. I AM NOT DRUNK! Look! I haven't touched a sip and I am just *a little* tired of you constantly criticizing everything I do — I don't mean it. I'm sorry. I love you, darling. I *worship* you. But, really I'm not drunk. I swear I'm not.

BOYD. I'm drunk.

NESSA. Boyd, however, is drunk.

BOYD. Just a little.

NESSA. Just a little. Boyd is just a little drunk.

BOYD. *Une petite.*

NESSA. French! He speaks French! You are so sophisticated.

BOYD. Thanks.

ARLOC. Mother, there's someone —

NESSA. Boyd, you weren't supposed to open that!

BOYD. Merry Christmas, Arloc.

NESSA. THAT WAS LAST WEEK! God. What's wrong with him? What's wrong with you?

BOYD. *(Shrugs.)* Bad upbringing, I guess.

NESSA. You know Arloc, I've been thinking. There is something very skewed, *skewed I tell you,* about our relationship. I'm your mother. I have the paperwork and everything —

BOYD. Arloc, it's time for you to shit or get off the pot!

NESSA. Don't interrupt me, Boyd darling. Particularly with vulgar outbursts. I was saying, here I am your mother, BUT you act as if you were my mother! You've always taken care of me. Even when you were little and put me to bed. I used to like it. It felt cozy. *My mother,* your grandmother, *never* tucked me in! I think she hated me. I think she was jealous. But, you know you don't have to take care of me anymore. It's not your job. You're not my mother. Not really.

BOYD. Have you decided?

ARLOC. About what?

BOYD. The movie!? Will you or will you not —

NESSA. Did you follow my point? About motherhood, dear?

BOYD. Trust me, you're going to be wonderful together. And after *Long Day's Journey* we'll do *The Sea Gull!* And all the Shakespeare plays. We'll make dozens of movies!

ARLOC. What are you talking about?!

BOYD. We'll be like a studio! MGM on Central Park! I love it here. I don't just mean the apartment —

NESSA. Which could use redoing —

BOYD. You should see my apartment, it's filthy. And worse than that, it's empty. I mean there's furniture in it —

ARLOC. Mother, listen to me.

BOYD. Why don't you love me, Arloc?

NESSA. Arloc loves you, Boyd.

BOYD. I don't think so.

NESSA. He loves you.

ARLOC. I love you.

NESSA. He loves you.

BOYD. He doesn't show it.

NESSA. Oh sex, sex, sex! Get your ass out of the toilet for God's sake! We're not gorillas, we're not orangutans! What about art? Love? Music?

ARLOC. Where have the two of you been anyway?

BOYD.   We went out.

NESSA.   Boyd, there was absolutely no new information in that sentence.

BOYD.   Sorry.

NESSA.   We went out to get champagne. For the party. To take to the party. You can't go to a party — with angels and elves — empty handed. We would have been back sooner, but we were almost arrested!

ARLOC.   You were what?

NESSA.   Oh calm down! We weren't arrested. We were AL-MOST arrested. It was just a prank. We sneaked into the giant nativity on Fifth Avenue — I don't know what possessed us. We climbed over the rail and Boyd crawled into the crib — we ditched the plaster baby in a bush — and I was going to be The Virgin Mary, which given my background was blasphemous anyway, but she was bolted to the ground. So I was a wise man! It was fabulous! We must've been there longer than I realized — because I was focused on Boyd, who looked darling in the manger, offering my myrrh — and when I looked up, quite a crowd had gathered! There must have been three hundred people! All staring at us, eyes wide, mouths agape, just worshipping us — well, worshipping Boyd really. The congregation was transfixed! It was stunning! Then, all of a sudden this one man, who it turns out had been Boyd's stage manager at Radio City, shrieks at the top of his lungs, "Someone! Someone get the police! That baby, that Baby Jesus is a thief!" He was referring, it seems, to the fact that Boyd'd never gotten around to returning his angel regalia — and then there was chaos! Great swarms of people stormed the crèche! Wise men destroyed and paper maché angels stomped to rubble! Oh the carnage was fantastic! It was easy to get away in the fracas, I simply pummeled Boyd's accuser with a plaster camel. But, I tell you, never, absolutely NEVER has the conflict between the commercial and the Christian been made more graphic!

BOYD.   We got some champagne.

NESSA.   We got three bottles, but I used one to club a Roman — Boyd, darling, go put this one away before you do more damage, would you? In the fridge-thing?

BOYD.　Yes, Nessa. Whatever you say Nessa. *(Boyd exits.)*

NESSA.　I've made a decision, Arloc. I think we should go away.

ARLOC.　Go away?

NESSA.　We should go someplace warm. Someplace hot and beautiful. I think it would be good for you. You look very pale and I'm concerned about you, your health, your ... well, your health.

ARLOC.　We'll talk about it later.

NESSA.　No! No, no, no. We'll talk about it right now. The three of us. You, me and Boyd. Isn't he cute? Sweet really. On the beach, under the sun, by the water, doing nothing, baking and sleeping. Baking/sleeping, sleeping/baking. *(Carl enters, quite stoic.)*

CARL.　Nessa.

NESSA.　Aaaaahhh! IT'S THE OLD YEAR!!

CARL.　I thought you said she wasn't drinking?

NESSA.　Can no one see that I'm sober as a judge?!

CARL.　You look very well.

NESSA.　Why didn't you tell me? You should have warned me —

ARLOC.　You wouldn't shut up!

CARL.　I wanted to see you.

NESSA.　*(Attempting dignity.)* It's nice to see you too, Carl. It is, really, really it is. But we're all going out. We're going to a party. It's a theme party and you wouldn't fit in. The theme is happiness.

ARLOC.　*(Forceful.)* I told you she didn't want to —

CARL.　*(To Nessa.)* Can we talk please? *(Boyd enters.)*

BOYD.　Arloc! I demand some answers. I refuse to be tortured in perpetuity!

CARL.　You must be Boyd.

BOYD.　Who are you?

NESSA.　Boyd, this is my husband. I can't remember his name just now, but trust me.

BOYD.　Nice to meet you.

CARL.　Why are you dressed like that?

BOYD.   I'm an angel!

CARL.   I thought you were a Greek girl from a vase.

NESSA.   *(To Carl.)* We're going to a party, we're the guests of toy soldiers.

BOYD.   Arloc —

CARL.   Are you all insane?

BOYD.   *(To Arloc.)* Life could be perfect, here, in this house, the three of us.

CARL.   I'd like to talk to you, Nessa.

BOYD.   *(To Arloc.)* We can live forever, right here.

NESSA.   Everybody, hush! Carl's going to talk. Talk Carl.

CARL.   *(Pause, clears throat.)* I'd like an explanation.

ARLOC.   *(To Nessa.)* Should we leave?

NESSA.   I really don't care. Stay/leave, leave/stay. It's moot to me.

BOYD.   *(To Arloc.)* Do you love me, Arloc? I mean, you say you do —

ARLOC.   Please, Boyd. Not now.

CARL.   *(To Nessa.)* I'm entitled to fifteen minutes after fifteen years.

NESSA.   You're right. So sorry. Keep in touch.

BOYD.   *(To Arloc.)* I can't help you unless you love me.

CARL.   I've been very unhappy since you left.

NESSA.   Who's happy? *(To Boyd.)* Are you happy?

BOYD.   *(To Nessa.)* I wanna be Bergman or John Cassavettes! I want to be held!

NESSA.   *(To Carl.)* Boyd's been drinking. A terrible habit of which I disapprove. Bad, bad, Boyd!

BOYD.   *(To Arloc.)* I don't think you love me at all.

ARLOC.   *(To Boyd.)* Please be quiet.

CARL.   *(To Nessa.)* You made me happy. I thought I made you happy.

NESSA.   You were mistaken.

BOYD.   *(To Arloc.)* I need to know you want me!!

CARL.   What's wrong? I'll fix it.

NESSA.   *(To Carl.)* You never touched me!

BOYD.   *(To Arloc.)* You never hold me.

NESSA.   *(To Carl.)* You treat me like a child!

BOYD. *(To Arloc.)* I won't stay unless you want me! I won't stay unless you touch me!

ARLOC. *(To Boyd.)* I DO! ALRIGHT!? I WANT YOU! I SWEAR! I WANT TO HOLD YOU! I WANT TO BE INSIDE OF — *(Boyd is asleep.)* Oh God! He's asleep.

CARL. He's drunk.

ARLOC. He's ill —

NESSA. Alcohol affects him.

ARLOC. He's narcoleptic.

NESSA. Take him to bed and lay him down.

ARLOC. *(Tugging Boyd.)* Come with me.

BOYD. *(Waking up.)* Make love to me.

ARLOC. *(Walking him out.)* I will. *(Boyd and Arloc exit.)*

CARL. *(Threatening.)* I want you to come home.

NESSA. I want to be sixteen again! Disappointment is a constant companion.

CARL. You were happy.

NESSA. How *can* you stand there and have the temerity to tell me *I* was happy? I wasn't *happy*. Never been happy!

CARL. What do you mean?

NESSA. I want to start over!

CARL. We can.

NESSA. ME! I WANT! ME! I want to start over. I just want to start everything over. I've screwed up all over the place —

CARL. I love you!

NESSA. You never talked to me!

CARL. I love you!

NESSA. You never held me!

CARL. I LOVE YOU!

NESSA. Why?!

CARL. What?

NESSA. Why do you love me?

CARL. I don't know. I just do.

NESSA. Then that's your misfortune.

CARL. *(Begging.)* Come home.

NESSA. This is my home! I live here now!

CARL. Nessa —

NESSA. *(Backing away.)* I screwed *everyone*. Did you know that?

64

I did. I'm not proud, but I'm not ashamed.

CARL. I don't care.

NESSA. All the time. Behind your back.

CARL. I don't care!

NESSA. Friends of yours.

CARL. I don't care!

NESSA. People you play golf with!

CARL. I DON'T CARE!

NESSA. People you see every day!

CARL. I DON'T CARE!!!

NESSA. I CARE!! *(Arloc enters and watches, unnoticed.)*

CARL. I knew there were others and I knew they didn't matter!!

NESSA. ONE DOES NOW!

CARL. What?!

NESSA. *(Cruel.)* Can you believe it?! At this point. At this late stage! I have someone, for the first time, I am *in love!!*

CARL. Who?

NESSA. Boyd! *(Arloc reacts to this.)* I have Boyd!

CARL. That child?!

NESSA. YES! THAT CHILD!

CARL. No!

NESSA. HE CAME FROM NOWHERE AND RESCUED ME!!

CARL. Stop it!!

NESSA. THE MIRACLE OF MY LIFE!!

CARL. STOP!

NESSA. HE'S BEAUTIFUL AND PERFECT!

CARL. NO!!

NESSA. AND I LOVE HIM!

CARL. NO!!!!!!! *(Carl grabs Nessa violently. As she struggles, Carl kisses her passionately at length. The general lighting goes out, leaving Nessa and Carl in a very bright, isolated pool of light. A second light comes up on Boyd — he is U. His position makes it clear he has not re-entered the room. Rather, he has simply appeared. Nessa and Carl separate slowly, gently and Nessa is Adelle. She has a slight British accent and a stillness, a judgmental air.)*

NESSA/ADELLE. Whatever is wrong with you?

CARL. *(Still, disbelief.)* Adelle. *(The light on Boyd fades out.)*

NESSA/ADELLE.   Stop fighting. Please.

CARL.   Adelle.

NESSA/ADELLE.   You never fought and it doesn't become you.

CARL.   Oh my God.

NESSA/ADELLE.   Don't be afraid.

CARL.   Oh my God.

NESSA/ADELLE.   Listen to me. I can't stay very long.

CARL.   What do you mean?

NESSA/ADELLE.   I cannot be clearer.

CARL.   Adelle, why? Why did you go?

NESSA/ADELLE.   I don't know. I'm not God and not everything has a reason, Carl.

CARL.   That's not good enough —

NESSA/ADELLE.   It'll have to be.

CARL.   You were so young.

NESSA/ADELLE.   I know. I wasn't even thirty.

CARL.   *(Touching her face.)* Are you safe?

NESSA/ADELLE.   Of course. What could happen to me now?

CARL.   Did it hurt?

NESSA/ADELLE.   Not at all.

CARL.   I always worried that it hurt. I said nothing. No good-bye.

NESSA/ADELLE.   Why would you?

CARL.   I'm sorry.

NESSA/ADELLE.   For what? What do you think you did? Do you think that there's some blame? Do you think I wasn't happy? I was. And am.

CARL.   Oh.

NESSA/ADELLE.   I wish the children were more pleasant. But there's time. Now listen —

CARL.   I miss you.

NESSA/ADELLE.   I see that. But Carl, the years have turned to decades. Don't you think it's time for some perspective?

CARL.   I can't help it —

NESSA/ADELLE.   Try.

CARL.   I didn't think anyone knew?

NESSA/ADELLE.   Please Carl, you don't belong here.

CARL.   It's not your affair.

NESSA/ADELLE.   I've come a *very* long way.

CARL.   I love her.

NESSA/ADELLE.   Do you?

CARL.   I need someone!

NESSA/ADELLE.   Not Nessa.

CARL.   But —

NESSA/ADELLE.   They're just beginning here. You have no place. *(There is a pause, he realizes she's right.)*

CARL.   It hardly seems fair.

NESSA/ADELLE.   Go home.

CARL.   Alone?

NESSA/ADELLE.   You're not alone. I'm there. I'm always there. I never left.

CARL.   What?

NESSA/ADELLE.   Go home, Carl.... Learn to see.

CARL.   *(After a moment.)* Did I love you enough? *(Nessa/Adelle kisses Carl and he walks, slowly, out of the light. Nessa/Adelle turns away as the general lighting returns, revealing Arloc as he was.)*

ARLOC.   Where's Carl?

NESSA.   Gone. What did you hear?

ARLOC.   You ... and Boyd.

NESSA.   Oh ... I was lying, you know. To hurt him. I was lying because I didn't know what else to say. Not a thing in my head. Isn't that something. I was lying, about Boyd, I mean. You do know that? I'd never do anything. *(Arloc goes to the bar and takes, from a drawer, a Tiffany box. He hands it to Nessa.)* What's this?

ARLOC.   Happy New Year. *(She opens the box. It is a long strand of pearls.)*

NESSA.   Oh.

ARLOC.   I found a sock filled with loose pearls.

NESSA.   Oh.

ARLOC.   In Boyd's underwear drawer.

NESSA.   When?

ARLOC.   Last week.

NESSA.   I see.

ARLOC.   I know, I knew — I don't care.

NESSA.   I wanted to give you something.

ARLOC.   Why?

NESSA.   I was too young to be your mother. And I let other people raise you.

ARLOC.   I was relieved.

NESSA.   We should never have been friends. You should have been my child.... I wanted to give you something.

ARLOC.   Thank you.

NESSA.   *(After moment.)* Do you love him?

ARLOC.   I don't know.

NESSA.   He loves you.

ARLOC.   Maybe I do. I want someone. *(Turning away.)* ... I'm scared.

NESSA.   I know.

ARLOC.   Do you love him?

NESSA.   I didn't think so until I said it. It sounded true.

ARLOC.   What should we do?

NESSA.   *(After a moment.)* It's New Year's Eve. We should go to a party.... I spent twelve years in one miserable marriage, and fifteen more in number two, because I thought all the time. I was afraid of everything, poverty and old age, and tomorrow, and when you were very small I was afraid I'd drop you so I never picked you up. Things will work out tomorrow.

ARLOC.   *(Quietly.)* Or not.

NESSA.   *(Smiling.)* Or not. *(They embrace for a moment, then break.)* Let's get drunk, and swing, naked from street lamps.

ARLOC.   I'm afraid of heights.

NESSA.   *(Shrugs.)* Hold me.

ARLOC.   I might. *(A long pause.)* We're late.

NESSA.   Get him. *(Arloc exits. Nessa gets their coats. She sees the envelope on the bar and picks it up, then replaces it. Arloc and Boyd enter.)*

BOYD.   Did I miss it? Is it next year?

NESSA.   It's next New Year's Eve. You slept all year and look very refreshed. *(They put on their coats.)*

BOYD.   I really shouldn't drink at all. Don't let me sleep through it.

NESSA.   Boyd, darling, tell me, who *are* you going to kiss at midnight?

BOYD.   I'll kiss whomever's closest. *(They start out the door.)*

ARLOC.   Oh. The champagne. You find a cab, I'll get it.

NESSA.   It's going to be murder, getting one — I hope there's vodka at this thing — Do the toys drink vodka? *(Arloc exits into the kitchen.)*

BOYD.   What's the difference? You're drunk now.

NESSA.   I AM NOT DRUNK! Why does everyone think I'm drunk? I'M LIVELY! *(Boyd and Nessa exit. Arloc enters carrying the champagne. He is about to leave, but he stops at the table. He puts down the bottle and picks up the envelope. He holds it, studies it for a long moment, completely calm. Finally, He stuffs it into his coat pocket, then he grabs the champagne and exits quickly. Fade out.)*

END OF PLAY

PROPERTY LIST

Lipstick (NESSA)
Restaurant knife (NESSA)
Bottle of wine (NESSA)
Glass of wine (NESSA)
Cigarette and lighter or matches (NESSA)
Business card (NESSA)
Sealed letter (ARLOC, NESSA)
Coat (BOYD)
Pills (BOYD)
2 wineglasses with wine (ARLOC)
Crystal paperweight (BOYD, NESSA)
5 one-hundred dollar bills (ARLOC)
Several pieces of heavy rope (ARLOC)
Bondage chair (ARLOC)
Set of keys (ARLOC)
Drinking glasses (ARLOC, NESSA)
Scotch bottle (NESSA)
Letter opener (NESSA)
Strand of pearls (NESSA)
Bag of magazines (NESSA)
Bags from video store
Checkbook (CARL)
Bottles of champagne (NESSA, BOYD, ARLOC)
Tiffany box with string of pearls (ARLOC)

SOUND EFFECTS

Phone ring

TODAY'S HOTTEST NEW PLAYS

❑ **MOLLY SWEENEY by Brian Friel, Tony Award-Winning Author of** *Dancing at Lughnasa.* Told in the form of monologues by three related characters, *Molly Sweeney* is mellifluous, Irish storytelling at its dramatic best. Blind since birth, Molly recounts the effects of an eye operation that was intended to restore her sight but which has unexpected and tragic consequences. *"Brian Friel has been recognized as Ireland's greatest living playwright. Molly Sweeney confirms that Mr. Friel still writes like a dream. Rich with rapturous poetry and the music of rising and falling emotions...Rarely has Mr. Friel written with such intoxicating specificity about scents, colors and contours." - New York Times.* [2M, 1W]

❑ **SWINGING ON A STAR (The Johnny Burke Musical) by Michael Leeds. 1996 Tony Award Nominee for Best Musical.** The fabulous songs of Johnny Burke are perfectly represented here in a series of scenes jumping from a 1920s Chicago speakeasy to a World War II USO Show and on through the romantic high jinks of the Bob Hope/Bing Crosby "Road Movies." Musical numbers include such favorites as "Pennies from Heaven," "Misty," "Ain't It a Shame About Mame," "Like Someone in Love," and, of course, the Academy Award winning title song, "Swinging on a Star." *"A WINNER. YOU'LL HAVE A BALL!" - New York Post. "A dazzling, toe-tapping, finger-snapping delight!" - ABC Radio Network. "Johnny Burke wrote his songs with moonbeams!" - New York Times.* [3M, 4W]

❑ **THE MONOGAMIST by Christopher Kyle.** Infidelity and mid-life anxiety force a forty-something poet to reevaluate his 60s values in a late 80s world. *"THE BEST COMEDY OF THE SEASON. Trenchant, dark and jagged. Newcomer Christopher Kyle is a playwright whose social satire comes with a nasty, ripping edge - Molière by way of Joe Orton." - Variety. "By far the most stimulating playwright I've encountered in many a buffaloed moon." - New York Magazine. "Smart, funny, articulate and wisely touched with rue...the script radiates a bright, bold energy." - The Village Voice.* [2M, 3W]

❑ **DURANG/DURANG by Christopher Durang.** These cutting parodies of *The Glass Menagerie* and *A Lie of the Mind*, along with the other short plays in the collection, prove once and for all that Christopher Durang is our theater's unequivocal master of outrageous comedy. *"The fine art of parody has returned to theater in a production you can sink your teeth and mind into, while also laughing like an idiot." - New York Times. "If you need a break from serious drama, the place to go is Christopher Durang's silly, funny, over-the-top sketches." - TheatreWeek.* [3M, 4W, flexible casting]

DRAMATISTS PLAY SERVICE, INC.
440 Park Avenue South, New York, New York 10016 212-683-8960 Fax 212-213-1539

TODAY'S HOTTEST NEW PLAYS

❑ **THREE VIEWINGS by Jeffrey Hatcher.** Three comic-dramatic monologues, set in a midwestern funeral parlor, interweave as they explore the ways we grieve, remember, and move on. *"Finally, what we have been waiting for: a new, true, idiosyncratic voice in the theater. And don't tell me you hate monologues; you can't hate them more than I do. But these are much more: windows into the deep of each speaker's fascinating, paradoxical, unique soul, and windows out into a gallery of surrounding people, into hilarious and horrific coincidences and conjunctions, into the whole dirty but irresistible business of living in this damnable but spellbinding place we presume to call the world." - New York Magazine.* [1M, 2W]

❑ **HAVING OUR SAY by Emily Mann.** The Delany Sisters' Bestselling Memoir is now one of Broadway's Best-Loved Plays! Having lived over one hundred years apiece, Bessie and Sadie Delany have plenty to say, and their story is not simply African-American history or women's history...it is our history as a nation. *"The most provocative and entertaining family play to reach Broadway in a long time." - New York Times. "Fascinating, marvelous, moving and forceful." - Associated Press.* [2W]

❑ **THE YOUNG MAN FROM ATLANTA Winner of the 1995 Pulitzer Prize. by Horton Foote.** An older couple attempts to recover from the suicide death of their only son, but the menacing truth of why he died, and what a certain Young Man from Atlanta had to do with it, keeps them from the peace they so desperately need. *"Foote ladles on character and period nuances with a density unparalleled in any living playwright." - NY Newsday.* [5M, 4W]

❑ **SIMPATICO by Sam Shepard.** Years ago, two men organized a horse racing scam. Now, years later, the plot backfires against the ringleader when his partner decides to come out of hiding. *"Mr. Shepard writing at his distinctive, savage best." - New York Times.* [3M, 3W]

❑ **MOONLIGHT by Harold Pinter.** The love-hate relationship between a dying man and his family is the subject of Harold Pinter's first full-length play since *Betrayal. "Pinter works the language as a master pianist works the keyboard." - New York Post.* [4M, 2W, 1G]

❑ **SYLVIA by A.R. Gurney.** This romantic comedy, the funniest to come along in years, tells the story of a twenty-two year old marriage on the rocks, and of Sylvia, the dog who turns it all around. *"A delicious and dizzy new comedy." - New York Times. "FETCHING! I hope it runs longer than Cats!" - New York Daily News.* [2M, 2W]

DRAMATISTS PLAY SERVICE, INC.
440 Park Avenue South, New York, New York 10016 212-683-8960 Fax 212-213-1539